Deci Quality Management

Also available from ASQ Quality Press:

Making Change Work: Practical Tools for Overcoming Human Resistance to Change
Brien Palmer

Finding the Leader in You: A Practical Guide to Expanding Your Leadership Skills
Anton G. Camarota

From Quality to Business Excellence: A Systems Approach to Management
Charles Cobb

The Six Sigma Path to Leadership: Observations from the Trenches
David Treichler

The Change Agent's Guide to Radical Improvement
Ken Miller

The Change Agents' Handbook: A Survival Guide for Quality Improvement Champions
David W. Hutton

Office Kaizen: Transforming Office Operations into a Strategic Competitive Advantage
William Lareau

The Recipe for Simple Business Improvement
David W. Till

The Trust Imperative: Performance Improvement Through Productive Relationships
Stephen Hacker and Marsha Willard

Transformational Leadership: Creating Organizations of Meaning
Stephen Hacker and Tammy Roberts

From Baldrige to the Bottom Line: A Road Map for Organizational Change and Improvement
David W. Hutton

The Executive Guide to Improvement and Change
G. Dennis Beecroft, Grace L. Duffy, John W. Moran

To request a complimentary catalog of ASQ Quality Press publications, call 800-248-1946, or visit our Web site at http://qualitypress.asq.org.

Decision Process Quality Management

William D. Mawby

ASQ Quality Press
Milwaukee, Wisconsin

American Society for Quality, Quality Press, Milwaukee 53203
© 2005 by American Society for Quality
All rights reserved. Published 2004
Printed in the United States of America
12 11 10 09 08 07 06 05 04 03   5 4 3 2 1

Library of Congress Cataloging-in-Publication Data
Mawby, William D., 1952–
   Decision process quality management / William D. Mawby.
     p. cm.
   Includes bibliographical references and index.
   ISBN 0-87389-633-5
   1. Decision making.   2. Total quality management.   3. Industrial
management.   I. Title.

   HD30.23.M378 2004
   658.4'013—dc22   2004013968

ISBN 0-87389-633-5

Publisher: William A. Tony
Acquisitions Editor: Annemieke Hytinen
Project Editor: Paul O'Mara
Production Administrator: Randall Benson
Special Marketing Representative: David Luth

ASQ Mission: The American Society for Quality advances individual, organizational, and community excellence worldwide through learning, quality improvement, and knowledge exchange.

Attention Bookstores, Wholesalers, Schools, and Corporations: ASQ Quality Press books, videotapes, audiotapes, and software are available at quantity discounts with bulk purchases for business, educational, or instructional use. For information, please contact ASQ Quality Press at 800-248-1946, or write to ASQ Quality Press, P.O. Box 3005, Milwaukee, WI 53201-3005.

To place orders or to request a free copy of the ASQ Quality Press Publications Catalog, including ASQ membership information, call 800-248-1946. Visit our Web site at www.asq.org or http://qualitypress.asq.org.

Quality Press
600 N. Plankinton Avenue
Milwaukee, Wisconsin 53203
Call toll free 800-248-1946
Fax 414-272-1734
www.asq.org
http://qualitypress.asq.org
http://standardsgroup.asq.org
E-mail: authors@asq.org

∞ Printed on acid-free paper

To my beloved wife LuAnne and my daughter Briana.

Contents

Figures and Tables

Introduction

A forgotten process in modern quality management prevents many companies from reaching their full potential for improvement. Neglect of this process can mean the difference between success and failure for even the most industrious continuous improvement system, and has economic consequences that can reach into the billions of dollars. This forgotten process is not a minor component in today's business venture—it has production levels that outnumber those of all the car manufacturers, computer chip fabricators, and software generators in the world. These products are decisions!

Some decisions have clear life-or-death consequences, such as those made by a heart surgeon during a tricky triple bypass or those made by a battlefield commander in Iraq. Other decisions have dramatic impacts on the bottom line, such as those made by a corporate board committing billions of dollars to an acquisition. But there are untold numbers of other decisions that span a spectrum of levels of importance. These are the decisions that are made every working day by every employee, and they are absolutely critical to company performance. Each of these decisions may not, in itself, have earth-shattering consequences, but the sheer number of decisions cannot fail to have enormous economic consequences for the bottom line.

This book takes the novel approach that decisions can be treated fruitfully as products of decision processes. One improves the decision by improving the process that produces it. A wide array of proven tools and approaches to quality management of manufacturing processes can be immediately applied to the management of these decision processes. This book is a guidebook to how one can adapt the proven tools of total quality management (TQM) to decision processes. It shows the specific adaptations necessary for applying capability, measurement systems analysis, Six Sigma, and lean manufacturing to decision processes. This book is not a compendium of all available methods, nor is it meant to be the definitive overarching textbook on this subject. It has the more modest goal of serving as a guidebook or trail blaze detailing one practical path to achieving world-class decision process quality management. This book will cut and clear this trail by following the story of one individual's successful attempt to improve his decision processes. It is the sincere hope of the author that future travelers toward the goal of decision process quality management will be able to follow this well-marked path.

1

The Impact of Bad Decisions

DECISION SCENARIO 1: THE ACCOUNTING AUDIT

Imagine for a moment that you are the chief accounting officer for a major international firm. For the past four years you have been on long-term assignment auditing the activities of a major energy-trading firm. Over the years of working with your firm's executive staff, you have gained their confidence, and they feel as if you are part of their operation.

And things have been great. The company's market value has skyrocketed, and your fortunes have climbed right alongside it. It has meant a new house and a new car and a membership at the golf club. It is true that lately some of the initiatives have been a little ungainly, but it wasn't all that different from the ones in the early days that had worked out well. This company was worth giving a little flexibility in its actions. Loose ends can be tied up when the economy loosened up a little.

But you are not feeling so comfortable today. An urgent phone call at 6:00 A.M. from your office manager, Mary, took the edge off last night's fine meal of filet mignon and its accompanying bottle of expensive wine. Mary called with news that the head office in New York had issued a fax that requires your personal attention. The memo had clearly stated that all offices need to comply with all document retention policies immediately and completely.

You scramble to shave, dress, and rearrange the day with your wife. She has to rearrange, but yes, she can handle dropping your kids at their private school. You are amazed at the heavy traffic at 7:00 A.M. as you drive to the office. You notice that quite a few of the executive spaces in the parking lot are filled even now. The security guard sounds normal as he greets you with the standard "Good day, sir." Obviously the grapevine of office information has not penetrated to this level of the operation yet. You open the doors to your office complex and witness a frenzy of activity. Most of the staff is busy shredding documents and erasing disks. Mary greets you before you are more than a few feet into the office. She looks as professional and competent as always, but there is just a trace of urgency in her gaze. She hands you a file folder full of faxes and documents and asks if you want coffee. You say yes and enter your office. Through the broad corner windows, you see the sprinklers soaking the 14th green of the Executive Club golf course. The lush green lot stands in surreal contrast to the brown grass surrounding the fairways.

You open the file folder and faxes, and letters spill out onto the surface of your otherwise immaculate desk. The topmost message, sent from the home office in New York, instructs you to send copies immediately to all level 2 and 3 office staff. It is a simple statement that all offices must be brought up to compliance with company standards on document retention immediately. Only the two exclamation points that terminate the message serve to distinguish it from the usual dozen or so that arrive each month. Most of the time you can ignore or sit on these requests for a few days, but this one clearly has a different level of immediacy attached to it.

Mary enters and hands you a cup of steaming coffee. She comments that the staff is busy updating their records and shredding those that are classified in levels cc through ff. She looks at you for confirmation that this is in accord with your desires. You nod, and she reminds you that certain level bb documents can be accessed only through your account. She will shred them if you deliver them to her. She smiles a minimal smile as you thank her for her job well done. She departs, and you start up your laptop.

It seems like the computer operating system takes an hour as you wait for it to allow you to access the files. Finally, you are in. You scan the list checking that all the pertinent files are located in the one directory and that there are no half-finished drafts lying around in your temp areas. You hesitate an instant as your hand hangs over the F8 function key. You silently congratulate yourself on your foresight to have the IT staff code that particular shortcut key so that it would completely delete the files without any chance of recovery. You have heard of all kinds of technological ways to recover files that supposedly had been deleted.

You mentally review the company document retention statement as you deliberate. It says clearly that "all level bb documents must have a destroy date of current + 5 days only with the designated document holder responsible for compliance." But, since you are the designated document holder for this level, surely this means you can define what current means. You know these documents intimately, and some of them could be awkward in an inquiry. Everything is legal, of course, but an outsider wouldn't be familiar with all the background information and might read the wrong things into them. On the other hand, these documents are the only paper trail you have that shows the full history of the office decisions, and identifies key players at all levels of the organization. These documents might just be useful to you if the company executives decide that you might be a convenient scapegoat. What should you do? Slowly, you place your finger on the key and begin to exert pressure. . . .

Not all decisions are as potentially momentous as the one described in the preceding fictional scenario, but many critical decisions are made daily in modern business and industry. And although executive decisions tend to have greater potential impact, everyone makes decisions of one sort or another every day. In the scenario, the attention is focused on the final, big decision to delete or not to delete. But if one steps back and considers the process, one can see a whole sequence of smaller decisions that precede it and influence its outcome. In fact, one of the major lessons of this book is that the quality of decisions is determined by the processes that create them. It is only through meticulous improvement of these decision-making processes that one can ensure that all decisions, including the big ones, are likely to end up successfully.

In order to understand this dependence of the decision results on the process that creates them, it is instructive to examine the decisions that are involved in this scenario more closely. First, there is the decision by someone in the home office to send the overnight memo. Then there is the decision made by the executive assistant, Mary, to call you into the office early. There is the decision to comply with her request. And what if your wife decided that she could not drop off the kids today? What if you had not decided to create that special F8 complete-delete function and instead had to destroy the entire hard drive? If these decisions had been made with poor quality, the last decision might not even be possible. Or, if possible, it might not be feasible to make it in a quality fashion.

Each and every decision affects our own lives and the lives of others. Each and every decision is made based on the cumulative information that is available to the decision maker at the point of the decision. Each and every decision has some outcome or set of outcomes that help determine its success. And, although decisions are often characterized as right or wrong decisions, it is more likely a continuum of outcomes is possible, with results ranging from poor to excellent. And every decision is influenced by the decision maker's environment, both internal and external, and is bounded in time. And, of course, even making no decision at the moment is also a valid decision.

Although it seems obvious that decisions are important in all affairs, one must carefully drill into the subject to understand how we proceed with managing and improving the quality of decisions. After all, the very ubiquity of decision making makes it all the more challenging to develop a generic approach to studying decisions. In an attempt to develop more strongly the connections between decision processes and the more familiar manufacturing processes, here is another scenario that will be used as a consistent guide throughout this book.

DECISION SCENARIO 2: THE SHOP MANAGER

Suppose that you are John, the production manager of a small facility that makes extruded plastic coverings. If you wish, you can think of this as the best job you could get after your debacle in the accounting department in the previous scenario. It is 9:35 A.M. on a Tuesday, and you have just finished your typical set of morning meetings. All the fires are out or at least just smoldering, and you (as John) can turn your attention to some long-neglected capability and capacity improvement projects.

There is a sharp rap at the door. Without waiting for an answer, the best process technician in the shop enters the office and closes the door behind her. You have already seen Charlotte in at least two other meetings this morning, but it is not unusual for her to stop by for further discussion. As she takes a seat across from you, she seems to be searching for the right words. You wait, and finally she gets her tongue untied and launches into an energetic explanation of an idea she has for improving the performance of line 3. She says that the idea might sound a little risky at first hearing, but that she has been working it out in her head for a month now. She thinks that installing a closed loop feedback controller will boost output on line 3 by 25% and cut nonquality costs by half. It would cost about $80,000 total with around $50,000 of that amount to be charged as a capital investment. She realized that this is brand-new technology for this shop, but it has had a string of proven successes in other industries.

You settle back in your chair, peak your fingers, and gently blow on them. Now, line 3 is not historically your worst line but it is not your best either. You estimate that it would take at least a 15% improvement in the production from that line for six weeks straight to justify that kind of investment. You also know, as Charlotte does not, that the parent company has already warned that capital investment will be severely limited this year. You and the planning team have already proposed using your capital allotment for a more routine overhaul of line 2. But Charlotte's ideas usually pan out, and she seems especially eager about this one. You consider the various ramifications of your answer and then begin to tell her that she. . . .

Again, numerous decisions are involved in this scenario, along with the obvious one about the support of Charlotte's idea for the process modification. For example, there is Charlotte's decision to bring up her idea, and to do so on a calm day after the morning meetings. There is the decision of the company management to restrict capital investment. And there are decisions made in the background about the product lines and the production targets and scheduling considerations, and so on. The quality of the John's ultimate decision will undoubtedly depend on the quality of the contributing decisions. Although there are methods and approaches that can be used to affect the quality of the particular decision at hand, these tend to have a higher cost and require greater resource commitment than improving the quality of the decision process itself. By focusing on the decision, John can ensure quality upstream of the actual decision. And he can use well-developed and well-known tools to accomplish this.

Often when one is involved in a decision, the immediacy of the moment takes over, and later, one is convinced that the decision made was the only one possible. It is common for a decision maker to defend choices with the statement that a decision had to be made, and it was the best he or she could do with the information provided at the time. But the truth is that nearly every decision is characterized by a set of possible actions that could have been chosen. There is always a choice involved, and the process by which one makes that choice strongly conditions its quality.

John would benefit from reconsideration of the above scenario in this light. Consider how his decision might be different if Charlotte had approached him in the middle of a production emergency or had interrupted his presentation to upper management on the finalized plans for renovating line 2. Would the decision be affected if the air-conditioning was broken in his office or if Charlotte was hard to get along with? What if her last idea had not panned out, and there was still a residue of failure staining her? What if she had presented the idea with a 25-page report showing detailed costs and benefits estimates instead of the informal one-on-one meeting with John? What if the methods she used to arrive at her estimates were not completely in accord with company standards for evaluating projects? What if the annual budget had already been prepared, and adding this new project would require a complete reworking of it?

And what about potential outcomes? John can clearly see that there is at least $80,000 at risk, but there are normally all sorts of additional indirect impacts. On one hand, his decision is likely to affect Charlotte's attitude. If he dismisses her idea out of hand, she could become reluctant to offer up any new ideas in the future. If John does support her idea and changes the investment plan to accommodate the changes, there will be an impact on the shop performance. What about the loss of the potential benefits from overhauling line 2? And what if the improvement is larger or smaller than she projects? Perhaps even less directly, there are potential long-term effects on his career and on the bottom line of the business. Again, the decisions could have results that are excessive, deficient, or, more likely, somewhere between the extremes. Again, the decision process could be affected by the time frame, the persons involved, the environment, and many other factors.

As John ponders these issues he begins to draw some conclusions. First, all decisions have consequences or impacts. These impacts are typically multidimensional. There are some impacts that are well defined and measurable, and some that are less tangible. The full impact of a decision is the total of all effects that are caused directly or indirectly by the decision. He remembers from his training in quality management that this definition has a lot in common with the definition of quality loss. Quality loss is the total of all effects the product can have once it was delivered to the ultimate user or customer (Ryan 1989). The actual impact of quality on a customer is clearly a function of the innate quality of the delivered products in terms of their consistency and conformance to target specifications, but the specific value is affected by all manner of unpredictable variables that are determined by the environment and customer behavior. From his other forays into justifying projects, John knows that even when one is dealing with dollars and cents, many choices, however arbitrary, must be made. In his company some of these choices relate to the selection of the investment horizon, the cost to benefit ratio, and monetary equivalency computations. And for the less tangible outcomes, the method is usually very informal and without good rules.

THE STUFF OF WHICH DECISIONS ARE MADE

John does some research into the definitions of a decision. He finds that a decision can be defined as a choice between alternatives. There seems to be a distinction made between normative and prescriptive decision analysis. Normative analysis is a systematic attempt to understand and model the actual decisions made by effective decision makers. The prescriptive approach provides a preferred method of decision making that is characterized as statistical decision theory (Tummala 1973). Although John can see that this more mathematical approach might not match reality in all messy details, he decides to investigate this avenue more fully. In his readings he finds that a useful definition of a decision includes at least four features:

1. A set of alternative actions that are open to the decision maker

2. A set of states of nature that determine the outcomes

3. A unique value or loss for each pair of alternatives and states

4. A probability distribution on the states of nature

John finds he learns best by applying new concepts to concrete situations, so he tries to formulate a common shop control decision in this new light.

Charlotte's proposal concerns the modification of the current method of cutter control on line 2. Currently the production operator takes a periodic sample of material and, by reference to a control chart, decides on an adjustment to the machine setup. Charlotte's suggestion involves replacing the manual inspection and decision process with an automatic feedback loop. Trying to keep things simple at this point, John starts his investigation with a consideration of just this cutter adjustment decision. He wants to try out these new concepts on an application with which he is familiar. If it works with these problems on the borders of manufacturing and decisions, he thinks, it will be easier to see how they connect with more abstract decisions.

He can see right away that there are two decisions for this cutter adjustment decision: to adjust or not to adjust. The states of nature must relate to the states of the cutter process. If it is on target, he would probably not adjust. And if it is off target, he would indeed adjust. He envisions the on-target condition to be a normal distribution centered on target that fits inside the tolerance limits. Contrariwise he sees the off target as a similarly shaped distribution centered 3 mm high off the target. To summarize these assumptions and to set up for assigning the values that are required to complete this approach, he constructs a list:

State of process	Adjustment decision	Outcome
On target	Do not adjust	?
On target	Adjust	?
Off target	Do not adjust	?
Off target	Adjust	?

This looks reasonable, even a little elementary, but he continues with trying to assign outcomes to each combination in the list. He can see that there are many ways in which to do is this. The references that he consults suggest that one can use costs, losses, or, even better, utilities for this outcome. Apparently it is the consistency of the values that is of ultimate importance to the method. He estimates, roughly, the relative losses from each scenario. For example, no adjustment of an on-target process might still have some costs associated with it, but the loss compared to a baseline should be $0. In a similar manner he estimates that any adjustment takes two minutes of operator time, so at the very least it imposes an additional $10 on the costs. But the adjustment of an off-target process must be more desirable than the adjustment of an on-target process, so he rationalizes that false adjustment actually loses an additional $5 over and above the $10 for the adjustment action itself. Although this is somewhat arbitrary, he feels he can justify conclusions based on these assumptions. But it is the fourth combination that causes him the most heartburn.

He struggles with the estimation of the loss when he chooses not to adjust when the process is off target. Clearly this could have enormous consequences if the nonconforming product got delivered to customers, but quality inspections systems serve as a last line of defense in his company to reduce the probability of this kind of mistake. Rather than get bogged down in the details at this stage, he uses a number that is high enough to embody the effect on the customer and also the internal quality costs. He arrives at the table presented as Table 1.1.

Table 1.1   Loss table for a cutter control problem.

State/action taken	Do not adjust	Adjust
On target	$0	$15
Off target	$100	$10

John makes a note to himself to follow up with Charlotte to see if she agrees with his numbers. Maybe he can run other scenarios to check the sensitivity of his conclusion to his various assumptions. But, other than these small doubts, he is pretty satisfied that the numbers in the table do reflect the gist of the cutter adjustment decision problem.

The final ingredient that is required in the recipe for statistical decision analysis is construction of a probability distribution on the states of the process. That is, what is the probability of the cutter process being on target or off target? These two numbers have to add to one to be probabilities, so John concentrates on just one of them. He spends some time looking through old adjustment records and observes the operators in action for a time. He does not have any way to check how far off target the process is in each case, but roughly there is an adjustment of some size every other sample. So if these results are valid, the probability of being off target could be as high as 0.50. And this would likewise mean that the probability of being on target was an equal 0.50. John is amazed to see such a high instability in the process, but for the time being, he will use this estimate.

According to his references, a statistical decision analysis can enable him to convert raw estimates into a decision policy that will minimize the average loss. John notes that this does not mean that every decision will be correct but only that the average loss will be maintained as a good value. This is not exactly what John was hoping for, but he has found through experience that this is often the best guarantee one can get when statistics are involved. The procedure could be illustrated by listing the possible decision rules and their expected outcomes. Since his toy problem was so simple, he could see the best rule by simple inspection of the resulting expected outcomes.

One decision rule that occurs to him is the highly impractical one of never adjusting the process no matter what happens. In this case only the "do not adjust" column of the table is used. The average or expected losses are the losses from this table weighted by their probabilities of occurrence. That is, if one never adjusts, half the time the process will be on target and the loss will be $0. The other half of the time, the process will be off-target and the loss will be $100.

John would really like a method that guaranteed a correct decision with $0 loss every time, but upon reflection, he can see that this is impossible as long as some variation in the state of the process is possible. And he has to admit that having some loss is the realistic situation. So he continues with the computation of average loss for some other decision rules. Another easy one is the (also impractical) rule of always adjusting. Then the loss would be $15 half the time and $10 the other half, or $12.50 on average. This is a clear winner over the never-adjust decision policy, even if it is still not realistic.

John works harder to compute the losses for more realistic decision rules. In the approach that is used in the actual shop decision today, the operator takes a single sample and compares it to a prespecified control chart. If this single measurement is outside the control limits, an adjustment is mandated. If the measurement is within the limits, no adjustment is necessary. The actual size of adjustment is left to the operator's discretion and the operator can override the rule if he or she thinks conditions demand it.

John realizes that he needs to review his statistical process control knowledge to continue with his decision analysis. Specifically he refreshes his understanding of the probabilities of getting points outside the control limits, given his assumptions about on and off target cutter processes. When he gets into it, he realizes that this is simple because of the way control charts are standardized to be +3 and –3 standard deviations from the mean. So for this example, the pertinent probabilities are:

State of process	Control limits Location	Probability
On target	Inside	0.9973
On target	Outside	0.0027
Off target	Inside	0.5000
Off target	Outside	0.5000

John is now ready to compute the average loss based on the current decision shop adjustment decision rule. He secretly hopes that this rule will come out good in this new way of looking at decisions. He begins his analysis by listing the different scenarios:

1. Process is off target, point is outside; an adjustment is made.

2. Process is off target, point is inside; no adjustment is made.

3. Process is on target, point is outside; an adjustment is made.

4. Process is on target, point is inside; no adjustment is made.

He likes the modular way in which he has listed these options, since now it will be easy to plug in the probabilities and attach the loss values.

1. $0.5 \times 0.5 \times \$10 = \$2.5$

2. $0.5 \times 0.5 \times \$100 = \$25$

3. $0.5 \times 0.0027 \times \$15 \sim \$0$

4. $0.5 \times 0.9973 \times \$0 = \$0$

The two zeroes make this easy. The average loss is just the sum of $2.5 and $25, for a total of $27.50. John thinks something is wrong here. He rechecks his calculations several times but finds no error. According to this decision theory approach, the policy of always adjusting is superior to the control chart approach.

He knows that he made up some of the numbers. Could this strange result be due to some of those choices? He decides to recompute everything to see whether the process is more stable, perhaps with a probability of 0.90 of being on target. The results of this computation for the three rules are:

Never adjust: $10

Always adjust: $14.5

Adjust if point is outside: $5.54

Yeah! Now things are making more sense. But this result also means that the computation of the best decision policy is not as simple as it appears.

DECISION LOSS FUNCTIONS

John discusses his work on decision losses the next day with Charlotte. She asks him if this is related to the Taguchi loss function (Campanella 1999), of which she has read in quality management books. John remembers the concept from a quality engineering course he attended. The loss function is a way to measure the potential loss to society that can be caused if a poorer quality product is delivered to the customer. It is assumed that a product loses some performance as its characteristics vary from their target. John sees how this definition is similar to the one he derived for the loss from a decision process already. In real situations this loss function is generally unknowable in all its details, so the quadratic loss function is employed as an approximation. One assumes that actions that improve the situation under this approximate loss function will also do so for the more complicated real (unknowable) loss function.

John also remembers that the course instructor said that there are at least three important things to be aware of when using a loss function. First, the loss is a potential loss if the product fell into the hands of the user. The potential loss can be avoided by numerous preventive actions such as sorting or process control. Second, the loss is meant to be a population-based value. The specific loss that is achieved is a predictable combination of the product characteristics and the peculiarities of the individual user. Third, a product may have to meet several performance specifications, each of which is expressed by a unique loss function. In a sense, this is part of the approximation in which we assume the losses are generated separately by each performance feature. It is possible to extend the concept to multidimensional loss functions, but, since the purpose is approximation, this is usually not done.

Charlotte and John try their hands at extending this concept to decision processes. It is clear that the loss from decision is also a potential loss. It is also an easy step to see how decisions can also have multiple dimensions, each with its own criteria and unique loss function. And, yes, it is also clear that there is a distribution of possible values represented by the different states of the process. It looks to John and Charlotte like a perfect fit and gives them additional confidence that they are on the right track.

John tries the experiment of applying the Taguchi loss function to the cutter adjustment decision. He has already assigned a loss to the particular case of a 3 mm off target process. So it seems to be a matter of extending this to other off target cases such as 2 mm off target or 1 mm. He tries to summarize this relationship in a simple function. Because Taguchi loss functions are supposed to be quadratic, he uses Table 1.2 to describe the situation.

Table 1.2   Loss table for various deltas.

State/action	No action	Adjust to target
On target	$0	$15
Off target by delta	$100 $\times$ delta^2	$10

Pairing this table of losses with a simulated populations of discrepancies, of values of delta, yields a population of losses. For example, if these deltas come from a normal distribution of lengths with mean = 0.95 cm and standard deviation = 0.15 cm, it yields 1000 random lengths and 1000 unique deltas. Applying the appropriate loss taken from the table to each of

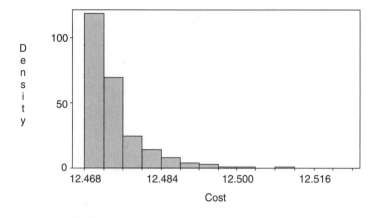

Figure 1.1   Distribution of decision losses under various deltas.

these 1000 results produces a distribution of losses as shown in Figure 1.1. This distribution is characterized by various summary statistics including the average loss = $12.47, as shown in Table 1.3.

As one last check on the suitability of this decision process loss function approach, John checks the impact of a clear process improvement on the computed losses. Specifically, if the variation in the process deltas is reduced then there should be a subsequent reduction in the calculated losses. If the standard deviation is reduced to .10 cm rather than .15 cm, then the resulting losses would have the summary found in Table 1.4, in which the average loss is reduced to $11.75.

John and Charlotte have convinced themselves of the feasibility of studying decision processes in a quantitative analytic way. They are not sure exactly how this approach fits in with the rest of the powerful TQM methodology, with which they have some experience. Specifically, they foresee a number of issues to resolve:

1. To identify and define decision processes

2. To measure the performance of decision processes

3. To set specifications for decision processes

4. To reduce work and lead time in decision processes

5. To assess capability of decision processes

6. To study the control of decision processes

7. To improve the quality of decision processes

8. To maintain the quality of decision processes.

Table 1.3   Summary statistics for decision losses with various deltas.

Moments			
N	1000.0000	Sum Wgts	1000.0000
Mean	12.4747	Sum	12474.7106
Std Dev	0.0062	Variance	3.826E–05
Skewness	2.7677	Kurtosis	10.3411
USS	155618.444	CSS	0.0382
CV	0.0496	Std Mean	0.0002

Table 1.4   Summary statistics of decision losses with decision process improvement.

Moments			
N	1000.0000	Sum Wgts	1000.0000
Mean	11.7551	Sum	11755.1062
Std Dev	0.3293	Variance	0.1085
Skewness	2.8011	Kurtosis	10.6127
USS	138290.868	CSS	108.3456
CV	2.8015	Std Mean	0.0104

But they are beginning to understand that this might not be such a difficult task after all. And they have high hopes that they will be able to uncover some real opportunities for improvement, because these kinds of processes have not been well studied. It is decidedly fuzzy as this stage, but John also has a gut feeling that it might be possible to shape Six Sigma and lean manufacturing techniques around the decision processes as well. John suspects that this decision process quality management might prove to be one of the best things with which he has ever been involved.

2

Where Decision Processes Fit into Quality Management

John knows that decision processes are not the only game in town when it comes to quality management activities in today's competitive company. Programs such as statistical process control, total quality management, and Six Sigma all apply powerful analytic tools to process improvement and control. These programs are used extensively in manufacturing processes, in measurement processes, and in design processes. Recently, the approaches have been adapted for administrative processes and even information flow processes (English 1999).

The losses claimed for poor quality can run easily into billions of dollars, and proposed remedies such as Six Sigma are credited with savings on nearly the same order of magnitude. There is no doubt that progress has been made using these tools in a comprehensive, coordinated approach. It is equally clear, however, that many programs do not measure up. Many well-funded and highly supported programs have failed or have at least been challenged. Though there are many reasons why such failures occur, one common denominator appears to be management support.

But why is it so? John draws a diagram of how a process management program might look (Figure 2.1). He sees that alongside the dominant hard physical manufacturing process are several shadow processes that work with information flow, administrative processes, and decision processes.

If decisions are embedded into the components of the operational processes, as he believes, improving these decision processes should directly improve the whole business process. Reversing this logic, he realizes that if these decision processes are in poor shape, this could bring about some of the difficulties that face quality management. But if these decision processes are critical, and if they impact the overall business so heavily,

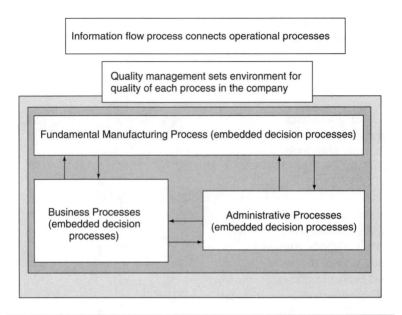

Figure 2.1   The generic quality process management approach.

why would an enterprise leave them unattended? He thinks more deeply about this. People in management roles make most decisions in an organization. Could there be some fundamental reason why management does not see that decision processes are part of the overall quality program? John can see that if there is some reason, perhaps it keeps TQM from being fully successful in many companies. John makes a list of arguments that managers might make about why they cannot benefit from the application of TQM to decision processes.

1. Decisions are unique.

2. Decisions are too complex.

3. Decisions cannot be measured.

4. Decisions cannot be predicted.

5. Decisions are an art, not a science.

6. We don't have time to make good decisions.

John is pretty proud of himself for the construction of this list, but when he shows it to Charlotte, she just snorts. She concludes that his list is just the same list that is always given as to why TQM can never work. John can see that she is right. These are the same barriers that were raised against TQM in the past and that are still being raised. While some might conclude that this means that the fight will be tough and long, John merely notes that it means that a successful path has already been established. He concludes that if he follows that path, success should be ensured. Again he cannot help but be encouraged by the neat fit of decision processes into the quality management fold.

Being a decision maker himself, John intuitively wants to control his own decisions. He feels, as most decision makers do, that scrutiny of his decisions only limits his options and has little chance of improving the result. On the other hand, he can see that quality methods are applicable to decision making, and he is aware of the positive benefits of TQM in production environments. Now that he admits to himself that he might be wrong, he sees that the system in place in his company reinforces this dangerous attitude. It is certainly not unusual for managers to fight any change in their methods. And since management at some level makes the rules, it is small wonder that managers have created a system that gives them almost total freedom in their decisions. John has seen during his career that it is the rugged individualists who are most often rewarded, especially those who shoot from the hip. John sadly realizes that very little is done to track the results of decisions. If there is no valid measurement of process results, how can anyone even hope to systematically improve them?

John expresses his concerns to Charlotte, and the two of them try to anticipate the arguments they will get from personnel if they try to implement a decision process management program on the cutter.

"We run 50 different product types on this line in a year," he expects the personnel to argue. "Each of these is unique because of raw material changes that Purchasing is always throwing at us. And then there are the temperature fluctuations in the shop, and the preventive maintenance had been cut back so the blade is never in good shape. We can usually make adjustments that can get the process running adequately, but we never have enough time to do it well. And the scales are a mess. They were all right when they were new, but now they are usually covered with oil and bits of shredded plastic. And some of the new operators do not follow the procedures well enough. They could use some discipline. So you could probably never put this under any kind of management. It has taken me at least 10 years to figure it out. We have so many big problems that it will be years before we're ready for a scientific approach."

Back in his office, John recognized all the standard arguments. It is the same resistance that all quality management programs have faced. Production personnel argue that their processes are too complex and idiosyncratic to formalize. Operators argue that no two production runs are alike. Engineers want to tweak and modify to their heart's content without any systematic method. Managers do not want their efforts to be quantified and classified. And no one has time to do it scientifically. Maybe there will be a time far in the future when this might happen, but for now, there are too many problems to overcome.

John also knows the history of quality management, however, and TQM is filled with examples of ultimate success once this initial resistance is overcome. He sees that what he needs to do is charge ahead with his plans, get some successes, and accumulate enough managerial support to give the program enough momentum to get through the bad patches.

It seems to John that the fundamental argument that the opponents of total quality management express is the fact that there are so many possible combinations of process conditions that there is no way to track all of them and predict or force a specific outcome. And since most process personnel think in terms of final products instead of processes, they also cannot envision a systematic way to improve these results. It seems clear that this is essentially the same argument that Charlotte and he are anticipating for the decision process management. Perhaps by analyzing the way in which one would counterargue for a manufacturing process, John will see how to counterargue for his decision processes.

A manufacturing process, such as the cutter process that lay behind the decision process of real interest to him, is subject to all manner of uncontrolled variations in inputs. The variations include differences in product type, material characteristics, and environmental conditions. The first step of a proper TQM approach (Garvin 1988) would be the definition of the process. He chooses to consider only stable operating conditions on one cutter with a production mix consisting of the most common products. Even with these simplifications, there are still clearly numerous possible combinations that can be invoked. This issue is at the heart of the opposition, as John sees it.

Suddenly, John has an "a-ha" moment. With a flash of insight he realizes that this very complexity provides the crucial argument for why the statistical approach will work. If the variations are small and nonrandom, there is no way to understand the dynamics of the process without understanding all the details. But if the complexity is great enough, and if the variations approximate randomness, it will be possible to predict the behavior of the ensemble of characteristics—that is, their distribution. A successful implementation of a statistical approach like TQM is aided by complexity, not impaired by it. The validity of the approach is threatened only if the distribution is not stable or consistent—that is, if it is not in statistical control.

John recognized that this is the critical ingredient in making this approach work. It is not the quality of individual products that he should seek to improve directly; rather, it is by improving the process that the quality of the results will be guaranteed indirectly and statistically. For the cutter process, this approach means that one does not try to correct each part or even reinspect it. Rather, one focuses on the process that determines the characteristics of all the products. And once this change of focus occurs, one seeks to keep the process stable and then improve its terms of width and placement with respect to target.

And how about the cutter adjustment decision process? Is this the same situation? John sees that in this case many of the inherent variations are identical to those at play in the manufacturing process. If anything, the decision process adds variability because of the extra steps of taking samples, weighing them, plotting them, and making the operator's final decision. So it should be even easier to make the argument that a statistical approach is the very thing for this process. He is ready.

He and Charlotte meet with the stakeholders of this cutter adjustment decision process, including operators, maintenance crews, and representatives of the supplier and customers. He starts with an overview of the problem and his belief that the application of quality management techniques can give them the leverage to make some substantial improvements. He emphasizes the team process in his presentation and attempts to make it clear that this is not a criticism of the way the operators are doing their job, but simply part of the more fundamental process improvement work that is being mandated throughout the company. Luckily, most of the team members have participated in previous statistical process control (SPC) events, so they are already knowledgeable and somewhat predisposed to the necessity of practicing TQM. However, as John allows them to voice their concerns, he finds that they are, true to form, expressing all the usual concerns.

John listens quietly and thoughtfully as they relate their concerns and questions. As anticipated, the crux is the perceived complexity of the decision process and the uniqueness of each decision. It is clear to John they are confusing the products with the process; if he can get them to recognize this, he can overcome their reluctance.

Presenting some of the examples that Charlotte and he have prepared, John shows how the variations can be described by a normal distribution and how this leads to the capability of the process. The majority of the team nods in agreement, since it looks a lot like what they have seen in their SPC training. But there are a few skeptical glares in attendance as well. He emphasizes the errors caused by the measurement process and the inconsistencies in the ways the operators interpret the results.

Although the conclusion is perfectly clear and undeniable to John and Charlotte, they can see that the audience's reaction is lukewarm. Some of them agree that it makes sense, but they are unsure because it is so unusual to study decisions in this manner. They ask, "Why hasn't it been applied to management decisions yet?" Perhaps if they can see a real application of the methods they will be better able to accept it. Although John would be overjoyed if the team accepted him at his word, he knows that this is just the opportunity that he needs to get his program rolling.

Later on in his office, John returns to one particular question raised in the meeting. He thinks he knows why this approach has not been applied to management decision before: because managers were defensive. Couldn't he correct this situation by applying decision process management to his own decisions? Indeed, he feels obliged to try it if he is asking others to experiment on their own processes. He thinks about the types of decisions he commonly makes. There are decisions about the budget, process improvements, resource issues, and shop communications. Some of these decisions are made quite infrequently, and even the most common ones number far fewer than those made by the operators in their cutter adjustments. Could these kinds of decisions also be successfully treated with the TQM approach?

He once again tries to reason through the problem by considering another manufacturing process. What would be an extreme case of a product that is so big and expensive and unique that it is produced in minute quantities? He hits upon the space shuttle as an example. He believes that only five shuttles have been built. But the fact that the process has only produced five items does not mean that it could not have created more. And if it did, there would be a distribution of possible space shuttles. And it should still be possible to improve the characteristics of this distribution by working on the process. It is possible then to improve the performance of the few products by ensuring that the whole distribution of possible products is good. Yes, it should be possible to apply TQM approaches even to processes that produce few products. like some of his personal decision processes.

John realizes that good procedures and methods can be applied to the quality of a particular part, in addition to the process approach. Usually these are known as inspection procedures. For example, one may inspect or test every single part. This can be an effective way to improve quality of the delivered product, but it usually is much more expensive than the process approach. And it is this same idea of inspection that appears to be at the heart of the usual statistical decision analysis approach. These appear to be methods to apply to each individual decision to decide whether it is good or bad. John decides to keep an open mind until he has a better chance to see the methods in action.

He recasts his process improvement decisions in the new light given by this process approach. He funds perhaps 25 such projects per year and has done so pretty consistently for each of the seven years he has been manager of this shop. But that means that this process improvement decision process has a total production of 175 products. That is a very low production rate compared to the operator adjustment decisions. He funds about 1 out of every 10 suggestions made to him, so this would bring the total number of decisions of this type to perhaps 1750. This is a reasonable number but nothing at all compared to the millions of possible projects that could be proposed! If he focuses on the decision process rather than the decisions themselves, he is not limited to just the few decisions that he has actually made. Rather, the process performance can be measured or estimated for the entire distribution of potential decisions. He is convinced that improving this distribution of all potential decisions should improve the few that are actually made as well!

John is really into this way of thinking now, and he doesn't stop with his own decisions. He thinks about managers who are on tiers above him in the company hierarchy all the way up to the corporate executive staff. They make even fewer decisions than he does in general, but these decisions tend to have strategic consequences. Does his argument extend to them and their decisions as well? He is sure that it does. Clearly, when one focuses on the possible decisions rather than on actual ones, TQM can be profitably applied to all decision processes, even the lofty ones made by the corporate brass. He sees that there is a potential problem to be faced in the analysis of such infrequent processes because of the scarcer data, but this does not mean that it is impossible. The more he thinks about these issues, the more that he realizes that he has to persevere with his attempt to establish TQM for decision processes precisely for these reasons.

He has the frightening thought that because decision effects are not studied and not tracked, the quality could be quite poor, and no one would really know. He thinks of at least four negative consequences of this exclusion of decision processes from the quality management program.

1. Decision quality is unknown and likely as high as 30% defective.

2. There can be no serious improvements until they are analyzed.

3. The only quality tool in use is costly repeat inspections.

4. The biggest impacts are likely to come from the worst offenders.

So, in the worst-case analysis, his company and others may be ignoring processes that are producing defective products, often with enormous economic impacts. In addition, there are no systems applied that offer any hope of continuous improvement. And as with applications in manufacturing, John can see that the ones who need the help the most are probably be the ones least likely to accept it.

John makes another note to follow up on the relationship of decision processes to personnel processes. He can see that a similar approach to the one that he is envisioning for decision processes may be just as powerful if it is applied in the world of objective settings and annual reviews. Here again the number of decisions is small, but the use of a process approach might result in real improvement in an area that is widely perceived as not open to scientific improvement.

The next question for John is how he can get the resources to give this new approach a go in his company. He thinks that the best way is to package it as an extension of the already strong quality management program. If he is successful in doing this, he will be able to piggyback on the momentum of this effort. After all, much of the training and procedures and methods are identical. It is only the application of these tried and true techniques to the relatively unexplored territory of decision processes that is novel. The real challenge will be to break down the wall that he expects upper managers will put up when he gets too close to their personal decision process. He also realizes that this attitude of acceptable ignorance can be causing huge economic losses without providing any mechanism for sustainable improvement. He can't wait to get started on some real applications.

3

The Identification
of Decision Processes

John is convinced that the time is ripe for some demonstration cases of his decision process management approach. The first step has to be the definition and identification of the decision processes to be treated in this fashion. He knows that the definition of a process is fundamental (Harrington 1991), and that a good definition goes a long way in ensuring good analysis.

Because he has found success to this point in relating the new decision processes to the more familiar manufacturing ones, he decides to explore what the definition of this kind of process requires. At an abstract level, a process is the transformation of a set of inputs into a set of outputs. For a manufacturing process such as a cutter, this is relatively easy to visualize as the set of machines, operators, and methods that turn a set of raw materials into finished goods. The production line of concern to John has an extruder and a cutter as well as a raw material loading system and a take-away system. It also has at least one operator. Since the operator can make adjustments, there must also be an interface to the process through adjustable machine settings. This set of physical elements is a process that converts input material into extruded tubing of a specified shape and size and then cuts them to the length required for ultimate delivery to the customers.

This description sounds straightforward enough to John—almost simple, in fact. But he can sense that as one moves from the abstract to the more concrete, one finds that the devil is in the details. For example, numerous environmental variables influence the operation. These include the ambient temperature in the work cells, as it affects the shrinkage or stretching of the product. Should these environmental variables be considered as part of the process for analysis purposes? It is clear that they are part of the physical system. And if one does include these variables, how does one characterize it? Perhaps the temperature of the work cell is exactly 72 degrees Fahrenheit for 23 hours and 55 minutes a day, but is a predictable 65 degrees the other

5 minutes. Or what if the temperature fluctuations are random, or are the result of an automatic feedback system like a thermostat?

Other issues arise when one considers the cutter itself. Should one consider it in its brand new state of six months ago, or in its current state, which includes any deterioration or wear caused by hard use and infrequent maintenance? Should one include that little quirky thing the cutter does upon startup that takes a few minutes of warm-up time to stabilize? And this is just one cutter. There are five other similar models, each associated with another production line across the shop. Should machine differences be taken into account in the analysis?

For any process, however familiar, John understands that its description will likely depend on the amount of time and energy that one uses in examining it. That is why it is so important to fully explore the possible process descriptions before a final form is chosen on which to base the analysis. There are many techniques to help one systematize this process so that omissions are less likely; Ishikawa (Ishikawa 1985) and process diagrams are two of the most common. Drawing or diagramming the process can lead to insights that are critical for the success of process definition. No matter how simple the process might look at first, a thorough analysis with an accompanying diagram seldom fails to illuminate some critical issues. For example, the creation of a comprehensive cutter process diagram (Figure 3.1) might lead to the discovery that the operator has been reading the pressure indicator incorrectly and has been running 10% low for four months now!

Now John tries drilling down to the cutter in question. He notes that it is just one component of the production line. The process consists of a conveyor belt that delivers cooled extruded tubing continuously from the extruder during a production run. The delivery is centered in the cutter and stabilized. The blade then makes its cut and retracts. The newly cut piece is released and transported away from the blade, and the new end of the bobbin is advanced a fixed amount of conveyor length. Characteristics of the incoming tubing, the ambient temperature, the pressure of the blade piston, and the speed of the blade movement all affect the cutting operation. Once released from the cutting process, the part is cooled and checked for correct length, weight, and aspect (no crushing or tearing allowed). The process is controlled by an operator who has control of pressure in the extruder vault based on a sample measurement of the weight and length of the cut product. John draws a rough process diagram that looks like Figure 3.2.

John realizes that this diagram can easily be made a great deal more complicated and detailed. Each of the blocks can be replaced by multiple blocks separating individual factors like wasted heat and lost material. And new blocks can be added for startup issues or to cover the few unusually viscous products. He wonders whether he should try to replace this static diagram with a more dynamic representation such as a simulation model or a

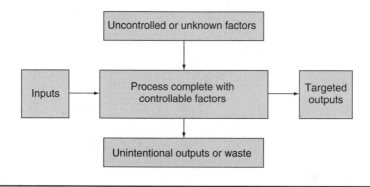

Figure 3.1   Generic process diagram.

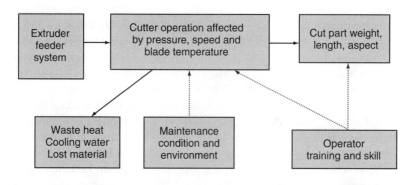

Figure 3.2   Moderately detailed process diagram for cutter.

feedback loop diagram. He saw a feedback loop diagram used effectively in a system dynamics conference he attended.

John feels a bit frustrated. It appears to be impossible to completely and correctly diagram or even describe the real physical process of interest. Can this be fundamentally correct? Does one need a completely valid diagram for the application of quality process management in an effective manner? After all, this is the diagram that is used as the basis for all further effort. But such a picture or chart or written description can never be identical to the real process. It becomes clear to him that what is essential is to draw boundaries and set limits, so that the model approximates the process in such a way that it could serve as a good working model of the true process. He is reminded of a quotation to the effect that all models are wrong but some are useful.

John concludes that it is an essential step in any process analysis, whether it is a manufacturing or a decision process, to abstract a useful

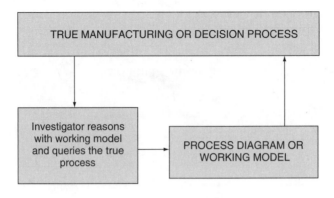

Figure 3.3 The use of the process model to guide investigation.

model of the true process. Analysis of this model will suggest real changes to be made to the true system. Further measurements enable one to refine or correct the old model; that can lead to further changes, and so on, iteratively. In this approach, it is the collection of data combined with a guiding theory or model that leads to improvement. A good model guides the analyst in his or her attempts to measure, control, and improve the real process. In a way, it is really this model of the process that is placed under TQM. The value of the TQM activities are interpreted and focused through the model process (Figure 3.3).

John sees that this modeling activity is also a process but decides to keep on track and ignore the implications of this conclusion for the time being. He consults several good books in which the art and science of modeling are discussed in detail. He learns that whatever the approach, he must have imagination along with detailed knowledge of and a feel for the process. Nearly all of the approaches also require iteration. And nearly all the experts on model building agree that the best models are those that are both accessible to the user and representative of the process.

In the case of the cutter, John begins the creation of a working model with a series of mental restrictions or boundaries that he imposes on the full-blown process. One restriction is to consider only the process as it currently exists. Operationally, *current* is defined as data collected after January of the present year. He also deems it more useful to use only steady-state runs, and to purge any startup periods or run anomalies from the database. Following further on this track, he restricts his process model to just the line 3 cutter and decides to consider the performance on only the large production runners. These large runners account for 80% of the total production by volume but only 50% of the product mix. He notices that each of these choices implies a restriction or an approximation and that any work that he pursues strictly with this model can be applied only to those processes. He tries to make good choices to reduce the complications of the model without sacrificing its usefulness. If he does this well, the facts that are learned on the approximate system will still apply, and will produce favorable effects when applied in the wider setting.

Once he has a good scope on the specific cutter process, John considers the implications for the generic situation. One expert (Casti 1989) suggests that it is best to start with a wide exploration of the process. Approximations can best be made when the overall lay of the land is known, so one has a better chance of achieving a globally pertinent model rather than one that has only limited applicability. The diagram or model should capture a wide variety of features and force the investigators to really think about the possible definitions of the process. Then, when they made the inevitable reductions and approximations, they may do so in an intelligently balanced way. As a rule of thumb, experts suggest that is usually better to begin with a full model and then make restrictions, rather than expanding a narrowly defined model. There are situations where either approach by itself can be best, and sometimes alternating between the upward and downward processes is needed to obtain a trustworthy fit. All the experts expect that the results will get better with practice and with adequate preparation of the participants.

John feels he is clear enough now on the intricacies of the process definition to consider it for the cutter adjustment decision process. The cutter adjustment decision process begins when the operator selects a sample product from the initial output of a production run. The work instructions state that the operator should wait at least two minutes for the manufacturing process to stabilize but can delay the sample even longer if there appears to be anything abnormal about the startup. He or she removes the sample from the output tray while the process continues to run. He or she places the warm sample in a ceramic sleeve, which carries it to a specially designed proprietary device that measures and weighs it.

The operator snugs the sample into the measurement device, reads the analog dial indicators, and records the measurement results into the computer program that stores results for traceability audits. He or she also visually inspects the sample for aspect. The work method allows the operator to remeasure the same sample if the device is giving erratic results. The operator then walks to another location and plots the values of the recently measured sample on separate control charts for weight and length. The rules of action state that if either plotted point is outside the control limits or if the aspect is unacceptable, the operator can choose to adjust the cutter. This adjustment is not set by any rule and is instead left to operator judgment and experience. The operator also marks the box of material if the sample is found out of control, in which case it must be scrapped. If this initial sample is in control on all counts, no further sampling is performed during that production run. If a sample is found to be out of control, the operator is instructed to wait at least 30 minutes before taking another sample. His or her actions are repeated for this new sample. If the resample continues five times and no points fall inside the limits, the entire run is sent to scrap. (See Figure 3.4.)

John knows that there are qualitative analyses that can be done on the basis of the diagram alone, but he considers the diagram to be primarily a guide toward the eventual creation of a mathematical model of the process. John has no illusions that he knows all the details of this process. Therefore any model based on his knowledge is necessarily incomplete. Each block in the process diagram can be expanded to an enormous level of detail if desired. For example, the weighing operation involves placing the sample on the scale platform, but this is affected by rectangularity of the cut edge of the sample. And the degree of this rectangularity is a function of the operator technique, the sharpness of the blade, and the viscosity of the sample. Or John can treat the more subjective process of the operator's decision about the stability of the production run. Clearly his or her thought process is built upon experience with the process and the particular product type being made. It also depends on the difficulty of taking a second sample and the awkwardness of the recording and plotting systems. And even the comparison of the points to the

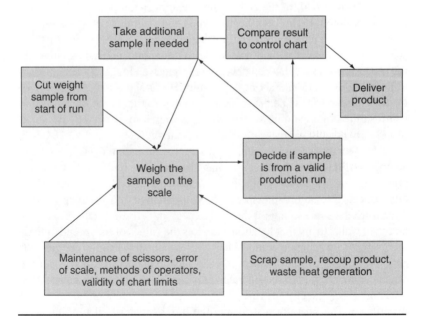

Figure 3.4 Cutter decision process diagram.

control chart limits is influenced by the method of computation by hand or by calculator, by any round-off rules that are applied, and by the resolution of the plotting instrument if it is performed by hand.

John decides to accept the model as it is, for the time being. He will attempt to apply appropriate restrictions and boundaries to it to turn it into a more workable model. The first restriction is to consider the decision process only on stable, current processes. Another restriction is to consider only the weight samples, since he knows from experience that almost all adjustments are made on this measurement rather than on improper lengths.

John understands the ramifications of making these restrictions. The restriction to stable processes may influence the distributions of data that he will consider, and the restriction to weight measurements can also affect this. The restriction to experienced operators acting on high-volume products will almost certainly limit the size and nature of the variations. The restriction to the current process may make it impossible to deal with long-term effects. John accepts all of these impacts as part of the interactive process of building a workable model.

The next step will be to populate his working model with details provided by data from the real process, but right now, he does not know exactly what measurements he will need or how he will obtain those that aren't readily available. He needs time to consider the measurement of decision processes. For now he assumes that data would be available, and he considers how this knowledge will affect his modeling procedure.

John knows that the weights are entered into a database, but he does not know how accessible the data is. For argument's sake, he considers this distribution to be a normal distribution, as most gurus of statistical process control (SPC) would have it. And there is likely to be some existing measurement systems analyses for this device that he can use. It will take considerable time and effort to collect all of the data and do the analyses, but it is clear that it can be accomplished. And the analyses should allow him to turn his model into a valid statistical one. He simulates the situation with some educated guesses as shown in Table 3.1 so he can get a feel for the steps of the process.

Table 3.1   Literal description of the model.

1. Weight distribution is normal with mean = 100 g and standard deviation = 5 g.
2. All samples have independent identical distributions.
3. The scale has 0 bias and repeatability standard deviation = 5 g.
4. The control chart has centerline = 100 and standard deviation = 5 g historically.
5. The costs are given in the following rules:
   —Each sample costs a fixed $10 in time and materials.
   —A recoup costs $250 regardless of amount.
   —Cost of delivered product = $2 × (true weight − target)^2.

This may have to be refined as better data becomes available but for now this is a preliminary working model on which John can practice.

1. Take first sample from normal distribution with mean = 100 g and standard deviation = 5 g and incur a cost of $10.

2. Measure this sample on a scale with a measurement error that is normally distributed with mean = 0 g and standard deviation = 5 g.

3. Take the resulting observation and apply the rounding rule.

4. Plot point on control chart and compare to a control chart with center line = 100 g and control limits at 85 g and 115 g.

   —If the point is inside the limits, pass products onto the next process and incur a cost of $2 × (true mean − 100)².

   —If the point is outside the limits, mark products and incur a cost of $250. Then return to step 1 to continue sampling until there is no more room to take a sample.

John can see a link between this process and his earlier work on loss functions. All he has to do is to try various possibilities for the process center to continue. For example, if there are only two equally probable choices at 100 g and 115 g, the cost computation can be simulated in this way:

Step 1: Pick a random value, such as 0.35689, from a uniform random number generator.

Step 2: If this value is less than 0.5000, assign the weight mean = 100 g.

   —If this value is greater than or equal to 0.5000, assign the weight mean = 115 g.

   —For the particular chosen value of 0.35689, the weight mean would be set to 100 g.

Step 3: Choose a random number from a normal distribution with mean = 100 g and standard deviation = 5 g; for example, a value of 102.44 could be the result.

Step 4: Simulate the measurement error by a random number drawn from a normal distribution with mean = 0 g and standard deviation = 5 g, such as –0.73.

Step 5: Add the simulated weight to the simulated measurement error to simulate the first observation that the operator treats; for example, $102.44 - 0.73 = 101.71$ g.

—Also incur a cost of $10 for the sample cost.

Step 6: Compare this value to the control charts limits 85 g and 115 g.

—If the value is inside, take no further samples and pass all material to the next post.

—Incur a cost $= \$2 \times (\text{true mean} - 100)^2$.

—If the value is outside, go back to Step 1 and begin with Sample 2.

—In this particular case the value is inside the limits and the cost $= \$2 \times (102.44 - 100)^2 = \$11.91$.

The total cost incurred for this decision process is $11.91 + $10 = $21.91.

John simulates 10,000 runs and arrives at a good idea of the distribution of costs. He finds that in his simulated set of 10,000 runs there is an average cost of $230.085. He tries a few what-ifs, since it is so easy to change the assumptions. When he sees the resulting changes in the average loss, he knows that this approach will permit a quality management program for his decision processes. But since he knows that his data are made up, he delays all real computations and conclusions until he can collect better data.

4

The Measurement
of Decision Processes

John begins to develop an extensive to-do list for himself in support of his effort to implement a decision process quality management program. He knows that he has to establish some indicators (Besterfield 2001) to track the success of his program. These indicators will justify quality decision process activities, their prioritization, and their usefulness. Given the notorious difficulty of getting face-to-face time with senior managers in his company, the indicators are likely to be the only thing that will get their attention.

INDICATORS OF DECISION PROCESS QUALITY

To this point he has been almost solely occupied with the cutter adjustment decision process, so John decides to alternate by considering a set of indicators with his own process improvement project decision process. As production manager he is often given proposals for process improvements. For example, just recently his top technician, Charlotte, came to him with an idea for implementing a new automatic feedback control to replace the operator-mediated system that is currently in place on line 3. His decision at this stage can take one of several tracks. On one hand he can accept Charlotte's idea as is and agree to fund the installation. The immediate impact of this decision will be the diversion of funds to this project instead of to other worthy projects, such as the overhaul of line 2 that is already part of the business plan. In addition, if Charlotte has misestimated, there could possibly be an overrun of the projected budget and, perhaps worse, a shortfall in capital funding. Or the project could turn out to be a bigger success that either of them dreams. Either way, if he shows Charlotte that he has confidence in her ideas, she might develop her skills and become a company leader.

John considers these impacts to be on a short-time scale. But other impacts are best expressed on a medium scale of time. There is a good probability that the decision will lead to the expected improvement in productivity for line 3, and this will enhance his image in the company and perhaps lead to an earlier-than-expected career boost. Also, if this improvement works it could proliferate to other lines, and the company could win big. And since this modification eliminates much of the operator involvement, it has ramifications for staffing reductions and allocations. But if the improvement doesn't pan out, this might have a harmful effect on his career and on Charlotte's performance as well.

And further out in time, this decision could be the first of a long string of failures that lead to Charlotte's resignation. Or the modification might prove so successful that John is appointed project leader to direct installation of the method on all the machines. And maybe the modification would result in a downsizing of the operators and all manner of personal ramifications. Indeed, if one considers an infinite time horizon the potential impacts can be astronomical!

John quickly realizes that the quality of decisions, like the quality of manufactured products (Gitlow et al. 1989) is the result of a multidimensional, complicated relationship. It depends on the characteristics they produce, of course, but it also depends on the conditions of use. An adequately performing automobile with no frills might be perfect as a first car for a teenager or for a financially strapped student, but it would be considered poor quality by a car aficionado. And the quality may change with time and information. The high-quality car—based on cost, drivability, and appearance—may suddenly lose quality when the driver has an accident and the safety system fails. Or a car might be considered high quality when gas is plentiful, then poor quality in an energy crunch, and then high quality in another time when gas is readily available again.

As variable as product quality is, John can imagine that decision quality is even more so. Decisions like the one facing a shop manager clearly have multiple impacts in monetary, psychological, productivity, and career development dimensions. It is also possible that the same decision can have opposite impacts on different users. For example, if the automatic feedback system suppresses manpower on the line, this would be a potential disaster for the operators. On the other hand, it might be a wonderful benefit for the company and for the manager's career in particular. And the quality of a decision may change with time. For example, the modification might fail to deliver the expected benefits. This might lead to Charlotte's being discouraged and going back to school for some more education. There she might come across a new concept that is even more productive than the original modification that she suggested. From Charlotte's point of view, the quality of the decision might easily change from highly negative to slightly negative back to an even more extreme positive.

As John considers the impacts of decisions, he realizes that, in addition to the features he already considered, that decisions have added complications in the ways that impacts are felt. A good decision in negotiating a deal on real estate on one side can have an opposite impact on the other party. If the monetary impact were defined as the sum of the two parties, it might come out at precisely zero every time (Hillier and Lieberman 1974). Also, one decision can readily be affected or even canceled by another decision later. A decision to deny Charlotte's request might at first appear to be a bad one if it destroys her confidence, but this could be more than overcome by later reversing the decision and giving her a raise. The sum of both impacts might be positive, negative, or zero, depending on when they are measured. In fact, it is this reversibility of many decisions that makes them so expensive. Powerful decision makers commonly spend enough money and resource to make sure their decisions prove to be right, no matter the cost!

The salient point for John is that proper boundaries or horizons must be chosen to define the impact of a decision. Some decisions have all their impact loading up front, and their criticality is clear from the outset, while others have gradually accumulating effects that are more momentous than their first appearance indicates. For the purposes of decision process management, more or less arbitrary boundaries must be drawn around the impacts. The purpose is not to capture all possible impacts exactly. Even if this were possible, it would still probably be necessary to employ an approximation or model that captures the right impacts in a useful way.

In John's case he is aware that company rules on evaluating projects will help him set some of these horizons. For example, the company allows evaluation horizons of three years maximum. And in some of the equipment replacement allocations a new policy based on life-cycle costs is being implemented. The company also provides a set of guidelines on acceptable benefits that can be entered into gain computation, such as material savings, labor costs, and operating costs. There are no provisions for evaluating and including morale improvements, strategic advantages, or even opportunity loss. But John knows that real decisions affect all these categories regardless of what the strict definitions are.

John agrees that for most business needs it seems practical to keep a relatively short time horizon, on the order of a few years. There is probably adequate data and knowledge to do this reasonably well as long as one sticks to tangible costs and does not stray too far into the "softer" potential benefits and costs. This will generally restrict the major impacts to immediate costs, loss of the value of the postponed other projects, and the projected benefits over the three years. Subjective risk or knowledge is not codified into the guidelines, but everyone knows that managers can often circumvent the system if they want. Most decisions expressed in this manner can be compared and revised in a regular fashion without disturbing the portfolio too much.

Once impacts are defined and their horizons identified, they can be used as the basis for action. If the decision has several potential alternatives, these impacts can be estimated under each alternative to compare their relative advantages. As a simple example, John analyzes a case in which there is no chance of failure to meet expectations and no uncertainty in estimates or costs. Then the decision to follow Charlotte's suggestion might have an expected productivity gain of $1,000,000 considered over three years. There is an initial project cost of $50,000 and a loss of opportunity from the other postponed projects, which is on the order of $400,000. Combining these numbers, it appears that the value could be around $550,000 three years from installation. The decision to stay on the original course and not follow Charlotte's suggestion might have a $1,000,000 potential productivity loss of opportunity, a $400,000 gain off of line 2 and only an immediate cost of $10,000 for an overall value of −$590,000. Or there might be another decision possible such as trying Charlotte's idea on line 2. On the surface it would look like this unconsidered option might have even more potential benefit. Of course, John realizes that every decision is made with a real chance of error and with the influence of uncertainty. So a better basis for comparison employs an average gain over the range of possible outcomes for each decision. Assume that the decision to implement the modification can have three outcomes. First, it might totally fail, meaning that there is $0 in improved productivity but still an initial $50,000 installation cost and a loss of opportunity cost. Second, the decision might be 50% successful for a $500,000 gain coupled with the $50,000 guaranteed loss and the opportunity loss. The third possible outcome might be the completely successful outcome that reaps the full $1,000,000 gain in the way that John considered. The average value of this decision could be computed using these three equally likely values. John could consider the success of the alternate decision to overhaul line 2 to be a probability as well, but he chooses to consider it a sure thing for the purposes of his analysis.

He computes the expected gain for the decision to follow Charlotte's advice as:

Chance of failure × gain under failure +

chance of middling success × gain under middling success +

chance of complete success × gain under complete success =

$.33 \times (\$0 - \$50,000 - \$400,000) = -\$148,500$

$+ .33 \times (\$500,000 - \$50,000 - \$400,000) = .33 \times (\$50,000) = \$16,500$

$+ .33 \times (\$1,000,000 - \$50,000 - \$400,000) = .33 \times (\$550,000) = \$181,500$

for an average value of $49,500.

He also computes the value of the decision to not implement the modification and to go ahead with the overhaul of line 2:

Chance of success $\times$ gain under success $=$

$1.0 \times (\$400,000 - \$10,000 - \$181,500) = \$208,500$

So the decision to reject Charlotte's modification is seen to be slightly more valuable. Of course, no "soft" benefits are included, but if they were incorporated into the decision then they may be enough to tip the scales in the favor of accepting the modification. In this manner it becomes possible to place value on a single decision. Thus the impacts of the many decisions that occur each working day can, theoretically, be rolled up into a single impact for all decisions that occur within a company. But the reality is that very few companies can track anything like this in detail, and still fewer managers have adequate time to do more than track indicators.

Although John is struck by the power of this decision analysis to treat difficult problems in a systematic way, he is careful to note that this is different from what he hopes to apply as decision process management. The process management approach strives to improve the decision process itself so that decisions will be better regardless of whether one uses this expected cost-based approach. That is, decision process management studies the factors that impact the eventual decision process and tries to reduce variations and center them. In this example, centering could mean removing any biases in the results caused by favoritism and reducing variability in the estimates of success or value. It could also mean speeding up the process of collection of the facts and figures. And it could include adopting a method like the one he is using to analyze results.

In John's shop, some common production indicators are production rate, quality throughput rate, cost per material unit, maintenance costs, and efficiency. For line 2 the automatic feedback system appears to be targeted to improving the production rate, but as it affects manpower resources it could also be aimed at cost per material unit.

A decision process can support the same kinds of indicators as the manufacturing processes. For example, one might track the cost per decision. The weighing of a sample costs $10, and a reduction in this amount through cost-cutting actions will also decrease the impact of the decision. Or the speed of the decision might be tracked. Because the samples are collected in a sequential fashion, there is only time for five such samples in a run. But if one could speed up the process, perhaps with an inline scale, then it would be feasible to take more samples during a production run. These indicators would fit right into the company's typical balanced scorecard administration (Hammer 2002).

Other approaches can lead to effective indicators on decision processes as well. These can be based on the decision outcomes themselves. For example, a manager might be tracked on all decisions that he or she makes in a month. The effectiveness of these can be evaluated and a rating given on the quality of each individual decision process. This rating could be a simple good or bad designation, an evaluation on a point scale or some continuous quantitative measure like the ratio of achieved value to potential value. More practically, it might not be possible or even desirable to track all decisions, but one could restrict the evaluation to only decisions of a certain minimum expected benefit. It might also be possible to simply sample the decisions that are made.

Whatever indicators John ends up with, he believes that their evaluation and tracking is primarily a statistical issue and can be effectively treated through the measurement of decision process capability. He concludes that the important thing is that these indicators should be carefully aligned with the overall business objectives and the key operating indicators of the company. The decision process management system should fit as neatly as possible within the overall process management structure of a company if it is to be successful and perennial. Otherwise, it will become more and more difficult to balance the activities and cost of decision process quality management with the activities of other initiatives. John believes that it should not be too tricky to make this connection for the decision processes in which he is interested.

John has two major objectives for the shop. One is an indicator of cost per unit delivered, and there is a target to achieve a 10% drop in this indicator this year. The second indicator is the total amount of scrapped product per month. The target improvement for this indicator is 5% versus last year's results. John chooses his decision process indicators to reinforce and support these business-based shop indicators and targets. He chooses an indicator of cost per decision for his planned improvements. This should reinforce the overall cost reduction effort. He already envisions that some specific process improvements that he has in mind may reduce the $10 fixed cost per sample to $8 by taking less product. Alternately an inline scale might be installed, taking costs even lower.

A second indicator that John considers for his decision processes is directly related to reducing scrap. He feels that a suitable indicator would be the percentage of falsely scrapped product resulting from bad decisions. His preliminary analysis has shown that this is affected by the variations in the true process weights combined with the rather large measurement error of the scale. A reduction of this measurement error should therefore result in less false scrap and eventually in lower volumes of scrap. But John can see

Another approach would be to cut 30 real products and measure their lengths very accurately, perhaps with a laser gage. In this case the laser gage is used to create a set of standards right on the spot. Again this approach is not perfect, and its validity rests on the ability to do the laser measurement under shop conditions without altering the material. Once the repeats are made, the differences between the measurements and the standards are computed and the average delta estimates the bias or inaccuracy of the photocell.

John reviews the definition of precision and finds that precision is the variation in measurements made under homogeneous conditions. This means the same part if possible, and the same environmental conditions as much as possible. It is meant to separate out as cleanly as possible the random error that is associated only with internal workings of the measurement device as different from the rest of the system of its use. For the photocell, this might be accomplished by taking a series of consecutive cuts with one production run under stable environmental conditions. The standard deviation of this set of runs can be an estimate of one source of measurement process error. But clearly this mixes production process variation with the estimate of measurement error.

Sensitivity of the measurement process is its ability to distinguish meaningful differences in the measured parts. For example, if two standards are different from one another by 1 mm, what is probability that the measurement will resolve them as different? It is the power of the device and its components to detect differences. One way in which to estimate this property for the photocell would to present differing standards to the device multiple times and evaluate how often the differences were detected at several varying levels of change. Again, this kind of test requires a standard or a set of standards and can lead to questions about how to perform the tests correctly.

The robustness or reliability of the measurement is also critical to its quality. This characteristic of measurement systems has two aspects. One is the ability of the device or measurement to proceed under unstable conditions. If the photocell, for example, is sensitive to vibration and to fluctuations in current, it cannot be of satisfactory robustness. The further ability of the device to remain usable through time is the reliability of the measurement. A reliable device would have a generally longer median lifetime than one that is less reliable.

Now John moves to consideration of the measurement of a decision process. In the case of the cutter decision process, at least two kinds of measurement systems are involved. On one hand there are the measurement systems that fall easily into the standard physical systems that can be handled under the usual approaches. These measurement systems include the scale on which the operators measure the various samples. There is also a length measurement involved and the qualitative aspect measurement. If one considers the scale as an example, one could do a measurement systems analysis exactly as one might do it for the manufacturing process evaluation. Since this measurement presumably would not be performed if the control decision were not being made, it is properly part of the decision process.

That is, one should run accuracy, repeatability, and reproducibility studies on the weighing process. For example, one might take a standard weight that is traceable to the national standards and weigh it 30 times under homogeneous conditions. The average difference is an estimate of the bias. If this bias is significant, then it would probably be corrected physically or, perhaps, mathematically adjusted.

In a separate study, one could have three appraisers measure some typical product samples three times. One could then compute the repeatability and the reproducibility of the measurement process. Comparing the combined effect of these two quantities, called gage repeatability and reproducibility (GR&R), to the normal process dispersion could ensure that the process variation should cause few misclassifications.

John is familiar with measurement systems analysis of gages like these, so he moves on to consider the processes unique to the decision aspects of the process. For example, in the cutter decision process one really wants to measure the actions that form the decision. These include the weighing process, the comparison of the measurement values to the control limits, and the operator's reaction to this comparison: scrap the product, pass it along, or take another sample. The operator plots the measurement value on the control chart and visually decides if the point is inside or outside the limits. The inputs to his decision process are the weights, and the outputs are the actions taken. There is no in-process measurement process to measure this process in the current system! Unfortunately, this is the usual case for decision processes. Just as they have been ignored in the impacts on the bottom line, so have they been ignored in adequate measurement systems.

John must therefore use a temporary measurement system arranged specifically for the decision process study. One possibility is to provide a second set of eyes to verify the scale reading and then verify that the operator makes the correct comparison to the control limits. An accuracy study could be done fairly easily by taking a standard weight and having an operator weigh it and record the resulting decision versus the control limits (Table 4.1). Since the standard value is known, one can check the results for correctness.

This is an attribute measurement gage as described here, but, of course, it could be done as a variables measurement study if the actual measured values are recorded and used. For an attribute gage, one is typically interested in things like the effectiveness = the number of right decisions × the total number of opportunities. In this example the operator made a misclassifica-

Table 4.1 Accuracy study for a decision process.

Part #	True	Meas	Part #	True	Meas	Part #	True	Meas
1	In	In	11	Out	In	21	Out	In
2	In	In	12	In	In	22	In	In
3	Out	In	13	Out	Out	23	In	In
4	In	In	14	Out	Out	24	Out	Out
5	Out	Out	15	In	In	25	Out	Out
6	Out	Out	16	Out	Out	26	Out	Out
7	Out	Out	17	Out	Out	27	In	In
8	In	In	18	In	In	28	Out	Out
9	In	Out	19	In	In	29	In	In
10	In	in	20	In	In	30	Out	Out

tion four times, so the effectiveness = 26 ÷ 30 or about 87%. Typically such a result indicates that work needs to be done in operator training to improve that percentage. It is also useful to measure the false positive rate = fraction of outs declared falsely (in this case is 1 ÷ 15 or ~7%) and the false negative rate = fraction of is declared falsely = 3 ÷ 15 or ~20%. Both of these results are considered large enough to require improvement.

In a similar fashion, this one operator study can be extended to multiple operators (Table 4.2). One does not have to have the true value in this case but often it is available for attribute studies without extreme difficulty.

The effectiveness of Joseph is 11/15 or 73.3% and for Eliza is 14/15 or 93.3%. Under AIAG criteria, Eliza's performance would be acceptable, but Joseph's performance would not be acceptable. False negatives and positives are only counted now if the operator is consistently wrong in the decision.

Table 4.2 Multiple appraiser decision measurement system study.

Part	True	Operator	Repeat1	Repeat2	Repeat3
1	In	Joseph	in	In	In
2	Out	Joseph	Out	Out	Out
3	Out	Joseph	Out	In	Out
4	In	Joseph	In	In	In
5	In	Joseph	Out	Out	Out
1	In	Eliza	In	In	In
2	Out	Eliza	Out	In	In
3	Out	Eliza	Out	Out	Out
4	In	Eliza	In	In	In
5	In	Eliza	In	In	In

Otherwise it is counted as a mixed result. In this example, there are two cases of mixed for part 3 with Joseph and on part 2 with Eliza. There is one instance of false positive when Joseph measures part 5.

John notes that the measurement process performance for this particular decision process is not acceptable and needs immediate improvement action. Perhaps the operators are rounding the values before they plot them. If so, a possible improvement might be better training of the operators. Or the problem may as simple as the scaling on the control charts. Or perhaps the control line is not marked heavily enough and a better printing might reduce errors.

John considers the possibility of automating the weighing in order to effect an improvement. Perhaps this is a fail-safe approach in which large values of weight lock down the system or where the operator is required to compute some kind of error check sum. Ideally the weight is taken and plotted automatically. This does not absolutely guarantee validity but would be likely to show much improved performance.

John considers as well the opportunity for measurement of the decision processes involved in his management of the shop. The accuracy of a decision by management can be analyzed in a similar way to that of an attribute gage. What is needed is a standard. But what is meant by a standard decision?

John knows that many production measurement studies for accuracy are done in a laboratory setting because it is infeasible to do it in the actual process. For example, it would be impractical to cut a standard multiple times in the cutter production process. The same can be true for a decision measurement process. One can create a decision situation of an artificial nature, that is, a lab situation, for which the correct answer is known. The manager can be presented with alternative scenarios that detail the pertinent facts of the decisions. Repeats can be handled as the same decision problem encoded in different words without any change in the expected decision outcome. These sets of scenarios can be posed repeatedly to the each manager. Each resulting decision can be tabulated and compared to the "true" decision accordingly. If the result is a yes/no decision, an attribute study approach is required. If the resulting decisions are quantitative, a variables study is possible.

John considers what such a scenario could look like. He, as manager of the shop, is given a proposal for a modification of the process. The alternate decisions are to accept the modification or to reject it. The process can be in a state in which the modification will produce a $100,000 benefit with probability 0.25 or in a state in which the modification will not work at a benefit of $20,000 with probability 0.75. The cost of the modification is $40,000. A normally poor performer offers this proposal. It involves a capital investment of a new device whose long-term impact is not well known. There is only one more month until the end of the budget year and 95% of the budget has already been spent. What should he decide?

The true answer can be generated by statistical decision theory or by any accepted process sanctioned and calibrated by the company. This could be reformulated with a different setting but with the same basic conclusion, such as: you are the project leader who must decide to spend extra money or a adding a feature to the new machine on order. Other reformulations can be constructed to increase the number of repeats that are considered.

It is also possible to estimate the repeatability and reproducibility errors of the managerial decision process in a similar fashion. Repeat decision scenarios can be constructed where the "true" answer is not assumed known. Instead only the consistency of the decisions is of interest. Reproducibility can be estimated by duplicating the study at other plants with other managers. It is also possible to treat reproducibility as differences in one manager's decisions through time or under nonhomogeneous conditions. These nonhomogeneous conditions could be simulated by placing the decision makers in a stressful situation as they make their simulated decisions or perhaps by rephrasing the scenarios in a confusing or unclear manner.

John could see that this laboratory or artificial testing of the decision process is certainly not the ideal way in which to evaluate the process. But this is also true of a manufacturing measurement system in which the standard has to be applied away from the process. There is an alternative way in which to set a standard for a decision. It might be possible to make the decision under real conditions and then use a standard method to assess its correctness. This is the preferred method for the cutter process as well. For the management decision process one could collect the pertinent facts, alternatives, and probabilities that affect each decision. Then a standard analysis like the expected loss approach could be applied after the fact to assign a best or true decision result. These conclusions could be checked against the actual results to assess the measurement accuracy or effectiveness.

The weakness in this second approach is that there may not be identical situations repeated in the actual decision scenarios. Thus it might not be possible to separate all the useful information that one might wish for. This is similar to running a short form study versus the long form or analytic method as described in the same AIAG manual. On the other hand, it does capture the real situations experienced in the shop more faithfully. There is also the chance that the true or best decision will not really be the best decision, since all necessary information may not be captured or be available. Again this is no different from the manufacturing measurement process situation in which the standard, when applied in the process, may not actually be the same value. This approach could also be applied without a standard by presenting the situation to other managers and using the consensus judgment as the true value.

UNCERTAINTY ANALYSIS

John knows a little about uncertainty analysis of measurement systems but does some additional research to convince himself that this approach also applies to decision processes. This turns out to be a different technique that is applied in parallel to the measurement system analysis. Uncertainty is envisioned as a type of guarantee on the probability that the true value is inside a prescribed interval of the form:

True value = measurement value +/− uncertainty.

Clearly this definition leads to all kinds of practical and theoretical statistical difficulties, but this guarantee is considered very useful when it can be given. Practically, the uncertainty for most measurement processes is produced in three steps.

1. A component uncertainty is estimated for every nonnegligible source of variation in a measurement process through a combination of data collection and expert opinion.

2. The component uncertainties are assembled through the use of a model into a total uncertainty; this is often the root mean square of the components.

3. The total uncertainty is extended to approximate a 95% coverage with the intention that the equation for true value given above holds for 95% of the values.

This concept of uncertainty can also be applied to a decision measurement process. For example, in the situation of the cutter decision, experts might first list all the possible sources of measurement uncertainty. Such a list might contain the following items:

1. Bias between shop standard weight and company standard weight.

2. Bias between company standard weight and national standard weight.

3. Bias between shop standard length and company standard length.

4. Bias between company standard length and national standard length.

5. Resolution of scale is 10 grams.

6. Control program calibration has limits of +/− 2 grams.

7. Control program calibration has limits of +/− 10 mm.

8. Bias in length measurement to temperature (1 mm per 10° C).

9. Variation due to different operators.

10. Variation due to different scales.

11. Variation due to different length devices.

12. Bias due to parallax on tape measure.

13. Variation due to operator fatigue.

14. Resolution due to rounding rules of operators.

For each of these items, the experts can estimate the effects caused by the various sources of uncertainty. These estimates might come from vendor specifications, from internal control procedures, from laboratory studies, or from engineering judgment.

Each estimate of uncertainty is recorded as an equivalent standard deviation, s_i, for each component that is deemed large enough to consider. John thinks there are probably only 10 items in the complete listing that he would consider large. If enough is known about the system to create a model for the combination of the component uncertainties, it should be used, but often an approximation is used. This approximation is that the components are all independent and that their variances should be added together. That is, the total uncertainty is often computed as the square root of the sum of the s_i^2. This number is assumed to represent a normal distribution of error around the measured value. Using the normal distribution, one next multiplies this total uncertainty by 2 to arrive at the extended uncertainty.

Often the value given for the uncertainty is not directly pertinent to a particular measurement. Part of the guarantee provided by the uncertainty computation, however, is the assurance that experts in the measurement system have taken a detailed, systematic look at the components of uncertainty. It is often taken as the starting point for new measurement system developments or for reconsideration of the decisions that are based on the results of these measurement processes.

For the managerial decision process John imagines that a similar approach to uncertainty analysis can be performed. The sources of uncertainty include:

1. Level of awareness of decision alternatives

2. Level of awareness of the process states

3. Knowledge of process probabilities

4. Knowledge of decision procedures

5. Reliability of the information

6. Knowledge of costs

7. Levels of stress

8. Levels of distraction

9. Poorly defined decision boundaries

10. Poorly measured decision benefits

11. Data collection errors

12. Calculation errors

Once a component uncertainty is established for each of these effects, John can assess them for inclusion in the overall total uncertainty calculation. He does not know of a proper model for combining the component uncertainties, so he figures that he will use the square root sum of squares procedure that is given as a fallback. Then he can use this overall estimate of standard deviation to construct an interval that tries to contain the true value with some reasonable, say 95%, probability.

John is convinced it will be quite easy now to apply measurement systems analysis to decision processes and provide a guarantee of their adequacy for the additional analyses he knows will be required. He expects to use these measurement systems in decision process capability analysis, in decision process improvement studies, and as the basis for his management system. He is ready to move on to the next task.

5

Critical Factors Affecting Decision Process Quality

Charlotte comes into John's office the next morning and shows him a book she has been reading. It is about statistical decision making (Lindgren 1971). She says it has some very interesting material but she can't quite figure out how it relates to the decision process quality management program that they are seeking to implement. She wonders if he can explain the relationship between the two disciplines. After scanning the book, John tells her that he is familiar with the approach and has been trying to understand its proper place as well. He repeats his example of the cutter adjustment decision for her. He explains the need for alternatives, for states of nature, for a payoff table, and for a probability distribution. He shows her the example average losses he has computed and how they can be varied through different choices of probabilities and other estimates.

Charlotte digests this information and asks a few questions of clarification. They both agree that the distribution seems to be what gives this its statistical flavor. And it is sufficiently general in nature that is should be applicable to diverse types of decisions. And if one complicates the approach a little by dealing with utilities and risk preferences, it looks very powerful. But they can also see that some of the difficulties would be hard for them to overcome. They had no good way to arrive at good cost estimates, and there were always more than a few possible decisions. To them it seems it would be next to impossible to have confidence in their conclusions because they would not have great confidence in their inputs.

John tries to explain that the methods suggest sensitivity analysis for this reason. Sensitivity analysis consists of varying the inputs and observing the impact of the changes on the results. It is especially crucial to identify changes in assumptions that cause flip-flops in the basic decision, say, from "accept the modification" to "do not accept the modification." But even this causes them difficulty because again it requires choices about the ranges of possible values for the inputs.

John goes on to say that the same approach can be effectively applied to more complicated situations as well. For example, there might be three optional actions in his case: (1) fund the improvement, (2) deny the funding, or (3) fund at a reduced level. And the most powerful application of the statistical decision theory approach seems to be in situations in which there are multiple steps or subdecisions that formed a decision tree (Lindlay 1985). Then one has all kinds of options, and the best decision is almost never obvious from casual observation. Additional what-ifs can be played out to assess the value of the purchase of expertise and control. He ends by saying that he is quite impressed with the approach and thinks that it has a lot to offer their effort to implement decision process quality management.

Charlotte can read John's face and suspects that, despite his apparently high regard for this methodology, there is something missing. When she asks him about it he admits it is true and goes on to explain his misgivings. He says that the thrust of statistical decision theory seems to be an optimal way of selecting an action or a set of actions in a policy. In this way it is setting a prescription for the decision-making process. It shows what the end target is, but does not show how to get there in a real process situation. For example, it assumes that the actions are well defined, but in real decision processes that may be half the battle of the improvement effort. And it also assumes that a probability distribution exists or could be established without great difficulty. But again the effort of collecting data and assessing probability distributions through decision process capability analysis is likely to a major consumer of program resources. And certainly this will be true if one wants to keep everything updated to current values. It is also likely that more than just the average value will be important to decision process quality management. He can imagine many cases where consistency in decisions would be more important than achieving the very best average value. And if the distributions and actions do not achieve the desired costs or results, statistical decision theory appears to have little else to say on how to make the improvement. Again, this is likely to be a critical activity for the quality management program.

John sees that the optimal statistical decision theory procedure can still be useful in at least three ways to them:

1. It can serve as a target or standard for studies.

2. It can be used like extra inspection to improve quality of individual decisions.

3. It can be used to prioritize improvement actions and validate gains.

But he does not see it unduly affecting the vast majority of the work that is facing them in their attempt to implement the decision process program.

Although the ideas are mixed to some extent, John himself thinks that the problem is that statistical decision theory seems to focus on the individual decision, not on the process, as decision process management should. In this sense it is an invaluable addition to other inspection management techniques such as reinspection, acceptance sampling, and fail-safes. He needs a method that can be applied to improve decisions no matter what the actual components of the individual decision are. He thinks that decision process management provides such a method.

CUSTOMER RELATIONSHIPS
FOR DECISION PROCESSES

John does think that their digression into statistical decision theory has reinforced the need to identify customers for the decision process and to better translate their needs into activities that are included in his decision process management program. He is pretty sure that a standard customer-supplier relationship (Berk and Berk 1993) is what he needs to deal with the first need and that quality function deployment will serve well to answer his second concern.

He and Charlotte consider the decision process of the operator as he or she decides to make a process adjustment or to let the process continue running without adjustment. The customers for this process must first be identified. But this identification process might not be as easy for decisions as for manufactured products. This decision affects the product quality itself. Therefore it seems reasonable that the customers of the decision are identical to the customers of the product. In this example, these customers are probably other manufacturers who receive the final products. For definiteness assume that there is one customer for the material processed on line 2 and that this customer is Plastic Toys.

Clearly in the case of an external customer there should be a contract with a detailed set of specifications for the product. This set of specifications will naturally include the target characteristics of the delivered product, such as length, weight, plasticity, and surface integrity. These specifications may include explicit consideration of the statistical variability of the products with respect to these characteristics. Hence there may be a requirement that 95% of the product meet the target specifications for each characteristic. There are very likely to be conditions on delivery dates and packaging as well. If the customer is internal, the same kind of requirements must be identified and understood by both customer and supplier. Some kind of feedback must be established to guide corrections if commitments are broken on either side of this relationship.

In the case of the cutter adjustment decision process John envisions that a set of simplified customer requirements might read like this:

1. Product weight must be within 90 g to 100 g.

2. Product length must be within 99 cm to 101 cm.

3. If more than 2% of any daily shipment is out of tolerances, it will be returned at cost +25%.

He keeps the list short for now but realizes that in real applications the actual requirements can be intricate and difficult to achieve.

Once the customer is identified and the customer-supplier relationship created, the supplier can take the next step of tracing back from customer needs to operational elements. Ideally one does not want to waste effort on anything that is not directly contributing to the customer delight. Of course, this ideal situation is rarely met in real manufacturing concerns and should not be expected to be satisfied completely for a decision process application either, but it serves as guiding principle. A systematic approach to this process of translating customer needs into supplier activities is embodied in the quality function deployment (QFD) tool (Berk and Berk 1993). The basis of QFD is to draw an array that specifies customer requirements on one axis, say the vertical, and supplier activities on the other axis. A relationship between the two axes is specified by a mark in the correct intersecting cell. It is important that there be at least one marked cell for every need and for every activity. Otherwise some needs are not being addressed or some activities are being wasted.

For the cutter adjustment decision process, John and Charlotte construct a QFD array that looks like Table 5.1, in which they assume that they have only a partial list of customer requirements.

In this example all actions are related to at least one of the customer requirements and all requirements are being supported by at least one activity.

Table 5.1 The quality function deployment array for the cutter adjustment decision.

Activity/needs	90g < weight < 100 g	99 cm < length < 101 cm	<2% out of tolerance
Use of scale	Yes		Yes
Graph of weight	Yes		Yes
Measure length		Yes	Yes
Graph of weight		Yes	Yes
Stop process	Yes	Yes	Yes
Scrap product	Yes	Yes	Yes

As an example of an unnecessary activity, the inspection for aspect is not required for any of the simplified needs. Similarly, if there is a need to guarantee plasticity of the material, no activity or measurement being performed supports this need.

It is reasonably straightforward to apply these quality techniques to the situation in which the quality of the decision is directly related to product quality. The decision can be treated almost as a complementary process step or machine setting. There are only two choices in this simple case, and both lead directly to measurable results. Many decision processes are amenable to treatment in this fashion, but there are others in which the connections might not be so apparent.

To explore a different kind of situation, John and Charlotte return to the process improvement decision. First, it is important to define the customers and their contracts with the supplier. Second, one can construct a QFD analysis to translate the customer requirements into supplier activities.

Customers are those who pay for the product and ultimately derive benefits from its quality. In the example at hand, the customers are the company managers who are involved in funding the improvement projects and maintaining the business with the external customers. They probably include plant managers and at least one higher level of managers at a corporate or divisional level. There are other individuals, often called stakeholders, who are affected by the decision as well. These include the shop personnel such as operators, technicians, and maintenance workers. Other stakeholders might include other shop managers who process the materials just before or after the shop in question. Stakeholders may also include central quality and technical support personnel who are interested in leveraging any improvements.

Restricting their scope to include only those members of the management staff who are directly in relation to John's shop, the pair imagines this customer-supplier requirement:

1. < 0.1% chance of catastrophic result meaning < $1 million loss.

2. < 15% overrun on budgeted amount.

3. Reduce cost by >10%.

4. Reduce cycle time by >5%.

5. >80% consensus on all decisions.

When the requirements are listed in this fashion, it is readily apparent that they are no different from requirements that might be placed on a manufactured good. The trouble lies in the fact that these requirements are usually not so explicitly declared for decision processes. This seems to be another deficiency that has developed from management's reluctance to systematically improve decision processes. The establishment of a customer-supplier contract is the remedy for this deficiency. It opens the lines of communication and forces both sides to take the time to understand their responsibilities and to seek remedies to any existing issues. For example, John might use the contract discussions to gain guarantees on engineering resources availability or to gain permission to hire external consultants.

With the customer needs specified, it is appropriate to do a quality function deployment check on the alignment of activities with customer requirements. The array in Table 5.2 describes this result for the line improvement decision process.

Table 5.2   QFD analysis of the line improvement decision process.

Activities/ needs	< 0.1% > $1 million	<15% overage	10% cost	5% time	>80% consensus
Operator input					Yes
Technical input			Yes	Yes	Yes
Steering team					Yes
Peer calls	Yes	Yes			
Consultant			Yes	Yes	
Read books			Yes	Yes	
Have review	Yes				Yes
Track budget		Yes			
Track returns	Yes				
Track cycles				Yes	

In this case all needs are connected to at least one activity and, likewise, each activity is in support of at least one need. This QFD analysis is a check for sufficiency and necessity of actions from a broad view. Any obvious hole should be addressed, but there is no guarantee that adequate resources will be targeted to the right needs.

John thinks these preliminary analyses are critical to establishing a decision quality process management program for company decisions. They set the stage for further efforts to analyze and characterize the statistical behavior of the elements that contribute to and control the quality of decisions. For example, since the probability of the success of the projects was deemed critical, it might be one of the first elements of the decision process that undergo additional study via a decision process capability study. Or the existence of rushed decisions might entail a lean manufacturing study of the component of the decision process to cut the preparation and delivery time. Or since the shop manager's decision quality depends on the vagaries of budgeting and review, maybe the company can create a set of contingent decisions that depend on the actual amount of money or resources available for the review. In this way the process may be adjusted more or less automatically for the variations that are induced by the input processes that feed the decision process. John can anticipate that a version of algorithmic statistical process control (ASPC) can be effectively applied to decision processes.

6

Determining Decision Process Capability

Having completed the preliminary work, John and Charlotte are eager to start the activity they think might have the most immediate benefit, that of determining decision process capability. *Capability analysis* is the process of collecting and analyzing data for the purpose of characterizing the statistical distribution that results from a process (Ryan 1989). The capability of a process gives a guarantee that the process will, despite its many random and unpredictable variations, produce a high percentage of its products inside the tolerance limits. It is able to give guidance to a quality improvement program because of its separation of processes into capable and incapable. The analysis that accompanies the decision process capability analysis can also give clues and guidance about the causes of incapability, and this can be immensely valuable in its own right.

John and Charlotte decide to begin their work with the cutter adjustment decision process. They remind themselves that the process consists of an operator taking a sample after it is cut from a long run of extruded plastic. The operator determines a weight and a length and makes an aspect judgment. If all properties are within a set of control limits, no further samples are taken and all pieces are sent for delivery. If the first sample fails to be within the limits, the operator uses his or her experience to make an adjustment, perhaps with the help of maintenance personnel. Then the operator takes an additional sample and repeats the procedure. A total of five samples can be taken in this way, and if the fifth sample is determined to be outside the limits the entire lot of pieces is scrapped.

Decision process capability is the capacity of this process to produce decisions that have some predictable probability of meeting tolerances. This definition requires that a model be used to approximate the process that can be analyzed to give the required guarantee. In order to have confidence in this approximate process, it will be necessary to check that the process is stable and that it is single distribution, which is usually assumed to be normal. John and Charlotte list the various factors that can vary in this process with the help of operators, maintenance workers, and others with knowledge of the system:

1. The measurement error of the scale

2. The rounding error of the operator

3. The graphing error of the operator

4. The variation in true product weights and lengths

5. Adjustment made by the operator based on experience

The capability is the capacity of the process and as such is a characterization of every possible product that could arise from the process. It is fundamentally unknowable and can be estimated only by snapshots of data that are converted into indices such as C_p and C_{pk}.

After some investigation aided by the information services group, John is able to discover that only the measurements for the sampled units are recorded. He has in mind to collect at least 100 samples that are representative of the complete process and that are as randomly dispersed as feasible. This proves to be a problem when he looks at the available data. He spends at least 10 hours in several passes through the data in an attempt to separate the proper product types, operators, and machines to match the ones that he has set out in the process definition. He thinks he is going to have plenty of data even with these restrictions, but Charlotte reminds him that he is supposed to use only current and stable data. With this taken into consideration he just barely has the 100 observations, which he hopes will enable him to establish the capability of this decision process (Table 6.1).

Table 6.1 Raw historical weights from cutter adjustment decision process.

Obs	Run	Sample	Weight	Obs	Run	Sample	Weight
1	1	1	97	13	8	2	91
2	2	1	99	14	8	3	91
3	3	1	91	15	8	4	91
4	3	2	91	16	8	5	91
5	3	3	91	17	9	1	104
6	3	4	91	18	10	1	101
7	3	5	91	19	11	1	98
8	4	1	97	20	12	1	103
9	5	1	101	21	13	1	93
10	6	1	102	22	13	2	93
11	7	1	99	23	13	3	93
12	8	1	91	24	13	4	93

(continued)

(continued)

Obs	Run	Sample	Weight	Obs	Run	Sample	Weight
25	13	5	93	63	35	3	106
26	14	1	103	64	36	1	108
27	15	1	88	65	36	2	108
28	15	2	88	66	36	3	108
29	15	3	88	67	37	1	105
30	15	4	88	68	38	1	105
31	15	5	88	69	39	1	98
32	16	1	95	70	40	1	97
33	17	1	109	71	41	1	96
34	17	2	109	72	42	1	99
35	17	3	109	73	43	1	91
36	18	1	99	74	43	2	91
37	19	1	104	75	43	3	91
38	20	1	97	76	43	4	91
39	21	1	107	77	43	5	91
40	21	2	107	78	44	1	101
41	21	3	107	79	45	1	86
42	22	1	109	80	45	2	86
43	22	2	109	81	45	3	86
44	22	3	109	82	45	4	86
45	23	1	97	83	45	5	86
46	24	1	101	84	46	1	94
47	25	1	107	85	46	2	94
48	25	2	107	86	46	3	94
49	25	3	107	87	46	4	94
50	26	1	95	88	46	5	94
51	27	1	105	89	47	1	99
52	28	1	95	90	48	1	90
53	29	1	102	91	48	2	90
54	30	1	101	92	48	3	90
55	31	1	105	93	48	4	90
56	32	1	104	94	48	5	90
57	33	1	104	95	49	1	102
58	34	1	106	96	50	1	95
59	34	2	106	97	51	1	102
60	34	3	106	98	52	1	104
61	35	1	106	99	53	1	98
62	35	2	106	100	54	1	104

Figure 6.1 is a plot of the raw historical data in time order.
Figure 6.2 is an initial histogram of the raw historical data.

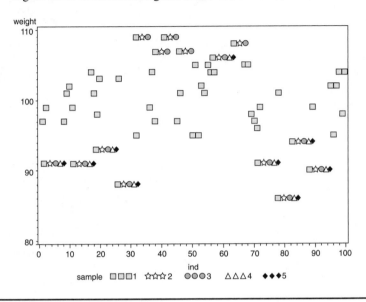

Figure 6.1   A plot of the raw historical data in time order.

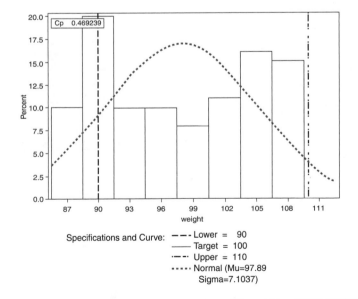

Figure 6.2   A histogram of the raw historical data.

These data are not exactly as John had hoped they would be. For one thing, the data certainly cannot, by any stretch, be considered a normal distribution. And they have an appreciable amount of product outside the tolerance limits. Both of these discrepancies present real problems to the analyst seeking to compute the capability of the decision process. There is even a hint that there are two modes in the distribution, implying that two distinct subprocesses might compose the process.

So John takes a more detailed look at his set of data in order to understand its limitations better. The time plot of the data clearly shows the multiple sample procedure. It also indicates that these additional samples often look like their predecessors and that real variation occurs more frequently between runs than between samples. And there are some points where it looks like further sampling should have been performed, but no further samples were recorded. Was the product scrapped, or did the operator forget to record the result, or what? It is not clear. Given the totally unsatisfactory nature of the process and the inadequacy of the supporting data, John concludes that he cannot use the historical data, and instead he needs to collect data in a special capability study. It is either that course of action or an attempt to correct the current data recording system so that months ahead it would provide adequate data. John chooses the more expedient way.

John asks Charlotte to perform this capability study while he goes about preparing for one that he hopes to run on the process improvement decision process. He provides a clear list of what he expects as deliverables from her work and arranges for some of her normal duties to be temporarily offloaded. Here is the list of deliverables:

1. Clearly understand the purposes of the study.

2. Clearly communicate these purposes to the operators.

3. Conduct a brainstorming session to assess possible sources of variation.

4. With the study team turn this wish list into a set of realistic conditions.

5. Plan to collect sufficient samples to see the targeted sources of variation.

6. Ensure an adequate measurement system for the decision.

7. Make a complete plan and have contingencies.

8. Run the study.

9. Do the proper analysis.

Each study will be unique and tailored to the process, the personnel and situation of the study. The results of each study should, however, characterize the process in a valid and useful manner.

Charlotte gathers a team of process operators, maintenance personnel, and technicians to do some brainstorming to identify important sources of variation that occur in the process. The team decides to collect data so that at least three operators will be involved, chosen randomly from the available crews. It is decided that the study can be repeated on each operator 10 times over the next month. Each segment of data—that is, an interval spent with one operator during one time period—will cover five runs made during that shift. If all goes according to plan, there should be five runs × 10 times × 3 operators for a total of 150 measurements, but the team realizes that there is likely to be some data lost. For each measurement an expert observer will check the proper decision independently of the operator. The operator will not be told of the expert decision but will use his or her natural procedure. For the study only, the data—consisting of the measured weight, the operator's decision, and the expert decision, along with the run, date, and other process variables—will be collected independently of what is entered into the database. Decisions about outliers will be made based on these data sheets. Notice that for the duration of this study there is effectively a new measurement system consisting of the expert observer. Doubts or questions about the performance of this expert will be verified in a separate measurement systems analysis.

The team and Charlotte realize that even though there are lots of advantages to conducting their decision process capability as a special study, there are some negative aspects. First of all, this is a different snapshot of a changing process, so it is likely that the data will be different. Second, the data are balanced, in that samples are taken from the same number of operators, the same number of time periods, and the same number of repeats. She knows that designed experiments can produce similar information but agrees with John that a simple study is likely to be more than adequate for this first study. Third, the presence of the expert will allow operators to know the correct answer, but will also probably affect the operator's performance since the operators are aware of the study. Fourth, the study is only over one month, so seasonal and long-term effects may not be experienced.

The actual study results are shown in Table 6.2.

Table 6.2 Corrected historical weights from cutter adjustment decision process.

obs	Date	Operator	Run	True	Delta	Sample	Weight
1	1	1	1	92.833	0.16676	1	93
2	1	1	1	92.833	0.16676	2	93
3	1	1	1	92.833	0.16676	3	93
4	1	1	1	92.833	0.16676	4	93
5	1	1	1	92.833	0.16676	5	93
6	1	1	2	99.193	−0.19274	1	99
7	1	1	3	101.092	−0.09173	1	101
8	1	1	4	101.167	0.83320	1	102
9	1	1	5	106.191	−0.19115	1	106
10	1	1	5	106.191	−0.19115	2	106
11	1	1	5	106.191	−0.19115	3	106
12	1	2	1	99.664	0.33610	1	100
13	1	2	2	98.987	0.01266	1	99
14	1	2	3	101.038	−0.03756	1	101
15	1	2	4	98.092	0.90804	1	99
16	1	2	5	97.488	−0.48784	1	97
17	1	3	1	106.886	0.11441	1	107
18	1	3	1	106.886	0.11441	2	107
19	1	3	1	106.886	0.11441	3	107
20	1	3	2	100.307	−0.30708	1	100
21	1	3	3	101.406	−0.40610	1	101
22	1	3	4	94.172	0.82805	1	95
23	1	3	5	100.730	−0.72965	1	100
24	2	1	1	92.131	−0.13122	1	92
25	2	1	1	92.131	−0.13122	2	92
26	2	1	1	92.131	−0.13122	3	92
27	2	1	1	92.131	−0.13122	4	92
28	2	1	1	92.131	−0.13122	5	92
29	2	1	2	102.854	0.14630	1	103
30	2	1	3	109.633	−0.63279	1	109
31	2	1	3	109.633	−0.63279	2	109
32	2	1	3	109.633	−0.63279	3	109
33	2	1	4	98.666	0.33426	1	99
34	2	1	5	98.811	−0.81139	1	98
35	2	2	1	98.517	0.48260	1	99
36	2	2	2	104.243	−0.24268	1	104
37	2	2	3	100.577	−0.57713	1	100
38	2	2	4	95.186	0.81419	1	96

(continued)

obs	Date	Operator	Run	True	Delta	Sample	Weight
39	2	2	5	93.363	−0.36312	1	93
40	2	2	5	93.363	−0.36312	2	93
41	2	2	5	93.363	−0.36312	3	93
42	2	2	5	93.363	−0.36312	4	93
43	2	2	5	93.363	−0.36312	5	93
44	2	3	1	100.487	−0.48734	1	100
45	2	3	2	99.617	0.38300	1	100
46	2	3	3	91.480	−0.48028	1	91
47	2	3	3	91.480	−0.48028	2	91
48	2	3	3	91.480	−0.48028	3	91
49	2	3	3	91.480	−0.48028	4	91
50	2	3	3	91.480	−0.48028	5	91
51	2	3	4	99.011	0.98877	1	100
52	2	3	5	97.541	−0.54115	1	97
53	3	1	1	110.190	−0.18963	1	110
54	3	1	1	110.190	−0.18963	2	110
55	3	1	1	110.190	−0.18963	3	110
56	3	1	2	96.024	−0.02393	1	96
57	3	1	3	93.697	−0.69691	1	93
58	3	1	3	93.697	−0.69691	2	93
59	3	1	3	93.697	−0.69691	3	93
60	3	1	3	93.697	−0.69691	4	93
61	3	1	3	93.697	−0.69691	5	93
62	3	1	4	98.534	0.46616	1	99
63	3	1	5	102.646	−0.64578	1	102
64	3	2	1	105.883	0.11719	1	106
65	3	2	1	105.883	0.11719	2	106
66	3	2	1	105.883	0.11719	3	106
67	3	2	2	99.280	−0.28013	1	99
68	3	2	3	103.693	−0.69272	1	103
69	3	2	4	98.843	0.15725	1	99
70	3	2	5	100.864	−0.86367	1	100
71	3	3	1	101.680	0.32019	1	102
72	3	3	2	102.463	−0.46317	1	102
73	3	3	3	111.563	−0.56315	1	111
74	3	3	3	111.563	−0.56315	2	111
75	3	3	3	111.563	−0.56315	3	111
76	3	3	4	96.771	0.22947	1	97

(continued)

obs	Date	Operator	Run	True	Delta	Sample	Weight
77	3	3	5	101.969	−0.96918	1	101
78	4	1	1	100.810	0.18968	1	101
79	4	1	2	95.456	−0.45576	1	95
80	4	1	3	101.154	−0.15414	1	101
81	4	1	4	101.588	0.41198	1	102
82	4	1	5	94.701	−0.70075	1	94
83	4	1	5	94.701	−0.70075	2	94
84	4	1	5	94.701	−0.70075	3	94
85	4	1	5	94.701	−0.70075	4	94
86	4	1	5	94.701	−0.70075	5	94
87	4	2	1	92.671	0.32858	1	93
88	4	2	1	92.671	0.32858	2	93
89	4	2	1	92.671	0.32858	3	93
90	4	2	1	92.671	0.32858	4	93
91	4	2	1	92.671	0.32858	5	93
92	4	2	2	99.057	−0.05682	1	99
93	4	2	3	100.306	−0.30638	1	100
94	4	2	4	96.801	0.19910	1	97
95	4	2	5	100.051	−0.05107	1	100
96	4	3	1	98.570	0.42955	1	99
97	4	3	2	89.781	0.21929	1	90
98	4	3	2	89.781	0.21929	2	90
99	4	3	2	89.781	0.21929	3	90
100	4	3	2	89.781	0.21929	4	90
101	4	3	2	89.781	0.21929	5	90
102	4	3	3	95.355	−0.35538	1	95
103	4	3	4	98.079	0.92058	1	99
104	4	3	5	106.800	−0.79970	1	106
105	4	3	5	106.800	−0.79970	2	106
106	4	3	5	106.800	−0.79970	3	106
107	5	1	1	103.850	0.14992	1	104
108	5	1	2	102.993	0.00705	1	103
109	5	1	3	103.182	−0.18203	1	103
110	5	1	4	102.151	0.84936	1	103
111	5	1	5	102.883	−0.88317	1	102
112	5	2	1	109.640	0.36031	1	110
113	5	2	1	109.640	0.36031	2	110
114	5	2	1	109.640	0.36031	3	110

(continued)

obs	Date	Operator	Run	True	Delta	Sample	Weight
115	5	2	2	107.213	−0.21294	1	107
116	5	2	2	107.213	−0.21294	2	107
117	5	2	2	107.213	−0.21294	3	107
118	5	2	3	95.627	−0.62710	1	95
119	5	2	4	99.943	0.05652	1	100
120	5	2	5	95.412	−0.41231	1	95
121	5	3	1	100.232	−0.23236	1	100
122	5	3	2	107.272	−0.27223	1	107
123	5	3	2	107.272	−0.27223	2	107
124	5	3	2	107.272	−0.27223	3	107
125	5	3	3	103.053	−0.05331	1	103
126	5	3	4	96.993	0.00730	1	97
127	5	3	5	101.190	−0.19039	1	101
128	6	1	1	105.153	−0.15307	1	105
129	6	1	2	97.963	0.03722	1	98
130	6	1	3	97.534	−0.53390	1	97
131	6	1	4	95.757	0.24317	1	96
132	6	1	5	92.406	−0.40622	1	92
133	6	1	5	92.406	−0.40622	2	92
134	6	1	5	92.406	−0.40622	3	92
135	6	1	5	92.406	−0.40622	4	92
136	6	1	5	92.406	−0.40622	5	92
137	6	2	1	99.638	0.36226	1	100
138	6	2	2	97.296	−0.29560	1	97
139	6	2	3	100.779	−0.77882	1	100
140	6	2	4	99.769	0.23115	1	100
141	6	2	5	100.637	−0.63651	1	100
142	6	3	1	101.174	−0.17378	1	101
143	6	3	2	96.139	−0.13878	1	96
144	6	3	3	103.928	−0.92764	1	103
145	6	3	4	110.787	0.21311	1	111
146	6	3	4	110.787	0.21311	2	111
147	6	3	4	110.787	0.21311	3	111
148	6	3	5	97.184	−0.18407	1	97
149	7	1	1	104.064	−0.06414	1	104
150	7	1	2	100.388	−0.38761	1	100
151	7	1	3	95.712	−0.71152	1	95
152	7	1	4	101.072	0.92816	1	102

(continued)

obs	Date	Operator	Run	True	Delta	Sample	Weight
153	7	1	5	98.223	−0.22280	1	98
154	7	2	1	96.090	−0.09022	1	96
155	7	2	2	102.394	−0.39370	1	102
156	7	2	3	105.486	−0.48560	1	105
157	7	2	4	106.465	0.53546	1	107
158	7	2	4	106.465	0.53546	2	107
159	7	2	4	106.465	0.53546	3	107
160	7	2	5	93.703	−0.70287	1	93
161	7	2	5	93.703	−0.70287	2	93
162	7	2	5	93.703	−0.70287	3	93
163	7	2	5	93.703	−0.70287	4	93
164	7	2	5	93.703	−0.70287	5	93
165	7	3	1	106.535	0.46454	1	107
166	7	3	1	106.535	0.46454	2	107
167	7	3	1	106.535	0.46454	3	107
168	7	3	2	96.491	−0.49060	1	96
169	7	3	3	100.547	−0.54673	1	100
170	7	3	4	99.020	0.97996	1	100
171	7	3	5	113.378	−0.37782	1	113
172	7	3	5	113.378	−0.37782	2	113
173	7	3	5	113.378	−0.37782	3	113
174	8	1	1	97.089	−0.08873	1	97
175	8	1	2	101.937	0.06287	1	102
176	8	1	3	97.609	−0.60942	1	97
177	8	1	4	111.781	0.21850	1	112
178	8	1	4	111.781	0.21850	2	112
179	8	1	4	111.781	0.21850	3	112
180	8	1	5	95.556	−0.55644	1	95
181	8	2	1	97.310	−0.30957	1	97
182	8	2	2	103.912	0.08832	1	104
183	8	2	3	104.930	−0.92953	1	104
184	8	2	4	96.936	0.06433	1	97
185	8	2	5	102.470	−0.46989	1	102
186	8	3	1	106.197	−0.19748	1	106
187	8	3	1	106.197	−0.19748	2	106
188	8	3	1	106.197	−0.19748	3	106
189	8	3	2	96.311	−0.31060	1	96
190	8	3	3	104.744	−0.74355	1	104

(continued)

obs	Date	Operator	Run	True	Delta	Sample	Weight
191	8	3	4	94.428	0.57167	1	95
192	8	3	5	99.642	−0.64157	1	99
193	9	1	1	103.594	0.40615	1	104
194	9	1	2	92.439	−0.43893	1	92
195	9	1	2	92.439	−0.43893	2	92
196	9	1	2	92.439	−0.43893	3	92
197	9	1	2	92.439	−0.43893	4	92
198	9	1	2	92.439	−0.43893	5	92
199	9	1	3	99.160	−0.15986	1	99
200	9	1	4	101.112	0.88820	1	102
201	9	1	5	103.417	−0.41687	1	103
202	9	2	1	100.025	−0.02531	1	100
203	9	2	2	98.261	−0.26051	1	98
204	9	2	3	104.894	−0.89379	1	104
205	9	2	4	101.405	0.59512	1	102
206	9	2	5	100.824	−0.82399	1	100
207	9	3	1	92.748	0.25184	1	93
208	9	3	1	92.748	0.25184	2	93
209	9	3	1	92.748	0.25184	3	93
210	9	3	1	92.748	0.25184	4	93
211	9	3	1	92.748	0.25184	5	93
212	9	3	2	103.340	−0.34013	1	103
213	9	3	3	96.921	−0.92066	1	96
214	9	3	4	92.393	0.60727	1	93
215	9	3	4	92.393	0.60727	2	93
216	9	3	4	92.393	0.60727	3	93
217	9	3	4	92.393	0.60727	4	93
218	9	3	4	92.393	0.60727	5	93
219	9	3	5	102.620	−0.62046	1	102
220	10	1	1	93.982	0.01763	1	94
221	10	1	1	93.982	0.01763	2	94
222	10	1	1	93.982	0.01763	3	94
223	10	1	1	93.982	0.01763	4	94
224	10	1	1	93.982	0.01763	5	94
225	10	1	2	98.795	0.20542	1	99
226	10	1	3	97.612	−0.61165	1	97
227	10	1	4	94.785	0.21545	1	95
228	10	1	5	96.565	−0.56480	1	96

(continued)

(continued)

obs	Date	Operator	Run	True	Delta	Sample	Weight
229	10	2	1	107.641	0.35850	1	108
230	10	2	1	107.641	0.35850	2	108
231	10	2	1	107.641	0.35850	3	108
232	10	2	2	100.300	−0.29974	1	100
233	10	2	3	99.262	−0.26178	1	99
234	10	2	4	101.344	0.65569	1	102
235	10	2	5	90.800	−0.79991	1	90
236	10	2	5	90.800	−0.79991	2	90
237	10	2	5	90.800	−0.79991	3	90
238	10	2	5	90.800	−0.79991	4	90
239	10	2	5	90.800	−0.79991	5	90
240	10	3	1	100.661	0.33922	1	101
241	10	3	2	96.182	−0.18239	1	96
242	10	3	3	104.478	−0.47807	1	104
243	10	3	4	99.373	0.62705	1	100
244	10	3	5	91.481	−0.48106	1	91
245	10	3	5	91.481	−0.48106	2	91
246	10	3	5	91.481	−0.48106	3	91
247	10	3	5	91.481	−0.48106	4	91
248	10	3	5	91.481	−0.48106	5	91

Figure 6.3 shows the time plot to assess stability. Figure 6.4 shows the histogram for assessing normality and capability.

This method of treating the delta between the best decision and a real decision separates the decision aspects from the measurement aspects of the process. In this way, by extracting the effects of the operator decision from the scale measurement error, it is apparent that this part of the decision process is visually much more stable and more normal, and the capability should give a confidence guarantee on the probability of being out of tolerance based on this part of the decision process. Further work can then focus on the scale measurement and eventually the variability of the incoming product. But it appears to Charlotte and later to John that the strict decision part of the process is not a concern compared to the tolerances.

While Charlotte finishes her special study, John plans a capability study for the process improvement decision process. He too forms a team that consists of other shop managers like himself, the quality director of the plant, and a representative from the corporate vice president of manufacturing. His team helps him select the appropriate data to use in terms of

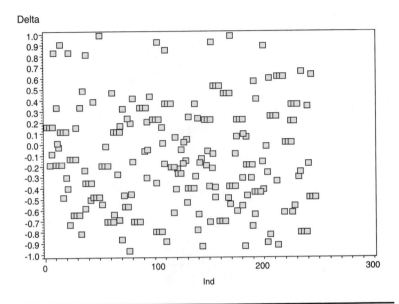

Figure 6.3   The time plot of the especially collected cutter data.

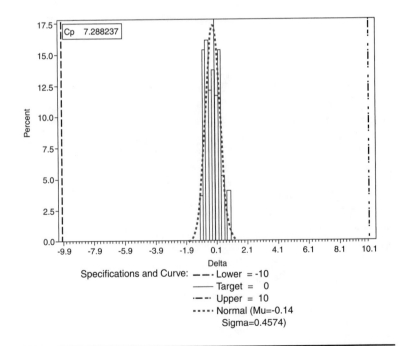

Figure 6.4   The histogram of the especially collected cutter data.

number of managers, the period of interest, and which abnormal conditions to remove. His biggest problem is that there doesn't seem to be any kind of measurement system readily available for this process. There is an accounting system, of course, but as long as the data meet legal requirements there is no need felt to track the success of the projects. And the project records he found in the system are scant and usually incomplete as to the exact nature of the project. So he and the team decide that they also need to make a special effort to collect adequate data through a decision process capability study.

The team identifies five sources of variation that they deem identifiable and important components of the decision process to be studied:

1. Date

2. Amount of request

3. Requester expertise

4. Type of improvement

5. Formality of request

The team thinks that time of the budget year as measured by data can affect the decisions, as well as the size of the amount requested. Additionally they suspect from experience that the expertise and experience of the requester is an influence that needs to be studied. And from his quick perusal of the few project records, John has a feeling that there is also a difference if the request is for software or training versus an equipment purchase. Finally, the quality manager fights hard to include a factor that focuses on the effect of the formality of the project proposal presentation.

The team almost reaches an impasse when they realize that there just aren't enough data to support an adequate study. A manager like John only sees about four process improvement requests per week. So it would take 25 weeks to get 100 data points, even assuming that all of these points met the team's stated criteria. It turns out to be one of newest shop managers who suggests that they simulate the decision process to speed the data collection. Perhaps they can generate decision scenarios and have the managers generate decisions from the scenarios. It seems feasible to do 20 or so of these kinds of scenarios a day, and thus it would only take a week to get 100 samples. Everyone understands that this is artificial, but if it is done well they believe it has good chance of producing useful results.

Once they get into the process of generating scenarios, the team finds that it is really quite easy to do. In fact, scenarios are so easy to create and to use as the basis for the simulated decisions that team members decide to raise their target number to 250 such samples. For each scenario the sources of variation are picked at random to cover most of the range of real decisions.

The manager is asked to read the scenarios and make a decision about the suggestion, given the details of the scenario. To check for consistency with real behavior, some real examples are scattered throughout the set of 250, with enough disguise to make them look new to the manager. To avoid decision fatigue, the decision maker is given the scenarios in a set of 25 over the course of three working weeks. Each scenario is assigned a correct answer based on a theoretical analysis done jointly by the statistics support group and the quality manager.

Here is an example of a scenario that is presented to the shop manager: It is November 3 and you are running at 85% of annual projected budget. The new technician on line 2 comes into your office out of the blue and suggests a good idea to reduce energy consumption of his line. This idea revolves around the retraining of operators to place the machinery at idle speed when product changes are being done. The total expenditure should be about 5% of the budget, so it is not too expensive. The project should have a four-month payback. There is a line of other employees waiting outside your office to present other options. No formal project plan has submitted for this work.

This scenario is presented as one in a set of 25 on day 1, followed by others like it. The statistical group and the quality manager review the decision and, applying the company guidelines, they assign a true or best decision of "yes." The difference between the manager's decision and the expert decision is computed and the number of discrepancies counted. The number of discrepancies actually found in the study is 1 of the 250 possible cases or 0.4%. If this is a normal distribution from a stable process then the equivalent C_p to produce an estimated 0.4% outside the limits will be 0.96, so it is very close practically to a capable process.

After reviewing their progress on the two decision process capability studies, John and Charlotte realize that decision processes can be just as complicated and hard to analyze as any manufacturing process and that initial capability studies will seldom show the characteristics that one would wish in a process. It is likely that, without followup work, the decision process will be unstable and this will lead to suspect estimates of capability. But, with insight and process expertise it should not be difficult to convert the initial process into one for which the estimate of capability is valid. This still could leave a problem, for the process may not be capable because of any number of reasons. They know that there are methods for efficient studies of decision processes, called design of experiments, that would help identify decision process improvements, and also methods like algorithmic statistical process control that could increase the efficiency and reliability of their decision processes.

7

Lean Manufacturing Applied to Decision Processes

As John pursues the improvement of the quality of the line improvement project decision process, he cannot help but notice that aspects of this process are related to its efficiency and flow. If he insists that process improvement suggestions be presented only at the monthly shop reviews, for example, then a good idea might be kept waiting during that time. To his production-minded eye this looks a lot like a raw material queue behind a bottleneck machine. He wonders how many of the steps in the process, such as the proposal, the request for more information, the justification, and the final review, should be considered value-added steps.

Obsessed with this idea, John drags Charlotte into the conversation. She says that she and Maxwell, the quality tech for that line, had been speaking about something similar just the other day. She and Maxwell had participated on the cutter adjustment decision process brainstorming team together, and it had struck them that many of the factors that had been raised in the session pertained to efficiency and flow more than to quality. For instance, they had quickly realized that the number of decisions was likely to be important to the overall quality of the final decision, but increasing that number would also slow the decision process down. After all, the operator could only take so many samples and monitor the process operation as well. So there is a built-in delay between each sample and between the initial sample and the final decision to reject the production of the run. That conversation had started Charlotte to thinking, but she hadn't had any time to follow up on her ideas.

John realizes that although these job responsibilities are primarily related to process quality, he should also seize the opportunity to improve the other aspects of decision processes. He has always felt that if he blames himself for every problem he sees, he will take it to heart and get things done. This attitude had worked very well for him so far.

He and Charlotte research the problem in some of the quality literature and find some excellent approaches that seem to fit their need closely. Charlotte is convinced that the concept of lean manufacturing seems most interesting. Lean manufacturing (George 2002) is a concept developed in Japanese manufacturing and exported to America along with many other quality innovations in the 1980s. The fundamental idea of lean is that all non-value-added steps should be removed from a process. For example, if product queues or inventories are created in the production of a product, these should be eliminated so that there is a continuous pull from customer demand through the process steps. Examples of systems that aspire to produce this ideal situation are KanBan systems, in which product production is regulated by card or messaging systems. There are also recommendations for shop flow arrangements and management.

She tries hard to convince John of the correctness of her viewpoint, but he tends toward the theory of constraints approach. The theory of constraints makes good sense to John because, although it too targets shop regulation as a method for improving efficiency of flow, it offers an approach that he thinks will likely be less disruptive to his shop. The fundamental concept behind the theory of constraints approach is to identify and overcome process bottlenecks as a means of improvement. John can envision a series of process improvements projects that will target each of these bottlenecks sequentially. But, he has to admit to Charlotte, she is convincing in her arguments, and perhaps a mixture of the two approaches can be the best approach of all.

John and Charlotte agree to create a team to try implementing lean manufacturing philosophy on the two processes with which they have experience and some reason to believe that significant improvements can be made. Since they pretty much have the process diagrammed, the team decides to measure the cycle time of the various steps that are identified. They list the process steps involved in the cutter adjustment decision process and estimate the cycle time for each one. Then they add a column in which they compute the actual time typically spent on that step. Most of this information is available from production records, but a few special studies are done to verify some of the steps that have not been under industrial engineering time study lately. Table 7.1 shows the table that the team creates.

The actual value-added time to make the decision is estimated to be between 14 minutes if the first sample is accepted and 72 minutes if the run's production is eventually scrapped. The elapsed time, due to transit time, to operator distractions, to poor equipment design, and other items, is actually between 69 minutes and 186 minutes. No wonder there is time for only five samples during a run!

The entire team, especially the operators, is astonished to see these results. Everyone had always accepted as fact that the decision process is

Table 7.1   Cycle times for the cutter adjustment decision process.

Process step	Cycle time	Elapsed time
Start up the run	2 minutes	10 minutes
Collect first sample	30 seconds	2 minutes
Weigh first sample	2 minutes	10 minutes
Round values	30 seconds	1 minute
Record values	1 minute	5 minutes
Plot values	1 minute	3 minutes
Make decision	3 minutes	10 minutes
Mark product	3 minutes	8 minutes
Repeat for next 4 samples	$4 \times 12 = 48$ minutes	$4 \times 39 = 156$ minutes
Scrap product	10 minutes	20 minutes

running quite efficiently, but the hard data show an entirely different story. The team is unanimous in its desire to reduce the amount of non-value-added time that is being employed. They begin to explore ideas for improving the situation. Some of the best ideas come from the operators. Since there are so many opportunities, Charlotte computes the efficiency of each step as the percentage of elapsed time that is occupied by the cycle time. (See Table 7.2.)

Table 7.2   Cycle times with added information for prioritization.

Process Step	Cycle Time	Elapsed Time	Efficiency	Ranking
Start run	2 minutes	10 minutes	20%	1
Collect sample	30 seconds	2 minutes	25%	4
Weigh sample	2 minutes	10 minutes	20%	2
Round values	30 seconds	1 minute	50%	9
Record values	1 minute	5 minutes	20%	3
Plot values	1 minute	3 minutes	33.3%	7
Make decision	3 minutes	10 minutes	30%	5
Mark product	3 minutes	8 minutes	37.5%	8
Repeat	48 minutes	156 minutes	30.8%	6
Scrap product	10 minutes	20 minutes	50%	10

So the start-up procedure, the weighing of the sample, and the recording of the values appear to be the worst offenders. But, as one of the team members points out, if a high percentage goes with a low actual time, the work may not be so important, and this should be taken into account. And then John, who knows that the budget is limited, adds that the easier fixes might also be good to consider first. The group readily agrees with these requests and uses a mixture of the three prioritizations to arrive at a smaller set of recommended actions. They will organize four dedicated events to work on for each of four identified steps.

The first event will focus on reducing the paperwork that the operators have to do at the start of a run. They usually let the process stabilize until they are finished with their paperwork before they get ready to take that first sample. The event will center on creating a reception sheet that will have all the information already printed and with an adhesive back. The operator will simply remove the sticker and place in on the reception form. In this way they hope to drop the elapsed time of the step to no more than three to four minutes.

The second event will focus on the weighing of the samples. Investigation shows that the problem is not the measurement itself but the fact that the sample is hot when it is removed from the process. It is too hot for the operator to handle safely when transporting it to the scale. The event will look into either cooling the product by dousing in water or providing some kind of mitt or glove to protect the operator's hand and allow a faster weighing. The team's expectation is that this simple action will cut the time at least in half.

The third event will deal with the recording and plotting of measured values. The operators complain that they have to find a marking pencil and need to remove the graph paper from the plastic covering that protects it against grime and dust. Ideas are generated for a new design that will allow the plastic to be a single sheet rather than an envelope that has to be removed. The idea of attaching the marker to the graph will also be explored. The hope is to reduce the times of both these steps by at least 30%.

The final event is designed to target the repetition of the procedure over five samples. This event is not thought to be as straightforward as the other three, so a series of studies will be undertaken during the event that will direct the improvement team to the correct actions. Some things that will be explored include the collection of all five samples at once, a reduction in the number of samples, and the question of whether the recording and plotting steps could be skipped for the follow-up samples. The actual gain will depend on the results of the studies, but the team is aiming for a 25% overall reduction.

In total, the team members think, they can shrink the total elapsed time from the original 69 to 186 minutes by 60 minutes in the worst case, from 186 to 126, and from 69 to 59 minutes for the best case. The actions should also decrease the risk generated from hot samples, relieve some frustrations of the operators about documentations, and provide for a traceability system with fewer errors. After these studies are run and the improvements are made, it turns out that some of the team's estimates of improvement were pessimistic and some optimistic. The total improvement over all steps is, perhaps surprisingly, near their estimate.

Charlotte and John are feeling pretty good about their first application of lean manufacturing techniques to their decision processes. They are so eager to start on the process improvement decision process that they are almost sorry to have a three-day weekend interrupt their work. John actually sneaks a little background reading in as he watches football that Saturday on TV. He cannot wait to get to the next problem.

The startup after the three-day shutdown and the start of a new month bogs down both Charlotte and John, but by Thursday they assemble the new team that was formed for the purpose of investigating the process improvement decision process. This team includes as members other line managers and plant personnel like the quality manager, Victoria. They are updated on the procedure, and they begin estimating the times associated with the steps involved in the process of making decisions about potential process improvement for production lines.

In this case, as opposed to the cutter adjustment decision, it is necessary to make lots of new measurements and to do more "guesstimation" of the times, since it is not common to routinely track this data for management decisions. John makes a memo to himself on his PDA that he should talk to the information systems group about creating data collection schemes for this kind of information. After three weeks of effort and a few short meetings, the team studies the results of the efficiency computations and rankings for the decision process steps. (See Table 7.3.)

They, of course, know that bureaucracy exists in their company, but they had no idea that it was of this magnitude and, worse, that they are part of the problem. They convince themselves that maybe it isn't as bad as it seems. Perhaps the cycle times for the steps are overestimates, because most of them were generated by expert opinion. But even if they are off by 100% the results are still awful. John and other managers feel a little embarrassed and are obliged to do something about this problem quickly.

Table 7.3 Cycle times for the process improvement decision process.

Process Step	Cycle Time	Elapsed Time	Efficiency	Ranking
Estimate gain	2 hours	10 days	0.83%	2
Estimate cost	2 hours	8 days	1.04%	4
Check resources	3 hours	15 days	0.83%	3
Prepare report	4 hours	5 days	3.33%	7
Edit report	2 hours	5 days	1.66%	5
Present report	20 minutes	45 minutes	44.44%	8
Modify report	4 hours	10 days	1.66%	6
Get sign-offs	1 hours	30 days	0.14%	1

Although John is more willing to spend money on the improvement of a decision process for which he is personally responsible, he still warns the team that the budget is limited, so they should select big hitters from this list of prioritized problems. There are some disagreements and discussions, but finally the group's members agree on three major efforts. Two improvements can be implemented in short measure, so they are scheduled to be accomplished in two events. The third deals with issues that will require more thought and toil. This is assigned as a project for Charlotte, who is freed from some of her daily tasks in order to address it.

One of the smaller tasks that the team implements quickly deals with modifying the approach to getting sign-offs. Currently this process involves a single copy of the proposal that is circulated in a specific pattern through the signers. Since it is likely that some of these executives are out of the office at any given time, it becomes a lengthy process to obtain all the required permissions. A new procedure is designed in which the proposal is circulated in parallel using multiple copies. Only the last signature (that of the comptroller) needs to be sequential. And they plan to implement an e-mail or phone message validation system as well. Thus there will be far fewer times when the report will be waiting on traveling executives. The team members estimate that these actions may cut the sign-off time from 30 days to a week at most. This will still leave a large percentage of non-value-added time, but it will nevertheless be a substantial improvement.

The second straightforward improvement idea that the team decides to pursue immediately is to construct a better way to estimate cost and gain. Upon investigation they discover that most of the time for these tasks is spent on obtaining the official numbers that have to be used in certain blanks on the proposal form. These official numbers are compiled each month by the financial department, but are not released until the 10th of the month in which they are to be used. So a lot of time is spent waiting for this official list to be distributed. The fix seems to be to adjust the proposal time so that old estimates can be used until the new ones were ready. This could be done by backdating the proposal, say from March to February, or by simply giving the date that was attached to the official numbers. This will cost almost nothing and can be implemented by some basic retraining of the administrative personnel.

The treatment of the third area identified for improvement is more difficult, and Charlotte has to do some extensive research to come up with reasonable answers. This involves creating a better method of checking resource availability. Some of the problem is administrative in that requestors don't get the right contacts quickly. Charlotte could easily design some fixes for this problem. More problematic, however, is the whole idea of project planning, wherein resources are shared among several projects. This is a sophisticated problem if one goes as deeply into it as Charlotte does. At first her penchant for mathematics leads her to consider scheduling software based on genetic algorithms, but when she sees the cost of these, she knows that she has to take a smaller step. So she decides to implement a priority and utility plan. She proposes that the resources be manned at such a level that they could handle 120% of the typical task loads. Then she creates a system that assigns a priority. Current projects or critical projects have complete control of resources during the duration of their project. If that resource becomes free or underused, it can be reassigned. Charlotte runs numerous simulations that show this system works at least 95% of the time using historical requests.

The overstaffing that is required by Charlotte's plan is a hard sell to management, but John supports the idea strongly. He shows the previous results of his work and presents the simulation results to everyone who might listen. He ends up sticking his neck out a little further that he intends, but it turns out to be worth the risk in terms of the gains that are produced and the confidence that is growing in himself and Charlotte. In the course of his pleading to a senior vice president, he gives what amounts to a guarantee of the success of this approach. John is worried at the possible consequences of his action, but this turns out to be one of the best gambles he has ever taken. Charlotte's idea accounts for a $2.4 million advantage when it is fully implemented 16 months later. The less ambitious actions also pay off with larger than expected reductions in decision processing time. It also convinces John to fund some further projects, which would target further gains in this area. These new projects are paid for with the gains made by the previous projects with a handsome amount of pure savings left over.

As he and Charlotte discuss their success one afternoon not long after the final presentation of the results, Charlotte asks eagerly whether he has any other special assignments for her. She is really excited about continuing this kind of work and wants to find assurances that she will not be going back to the same job that she had before. John has not really thought it out, but he too does not want to lose his chance to make real improvements like this in the company's decision-making processes. Charlotte's nudging is all he needs to admit this and formulate a plan for continued ambitious activity.

"Yes," he tells her. He has been thinking about another aspect of decision processes that they have left untouched.

"Sounds interesting," she replies. "What do you have in mind?"

He sits back in his chair and grins a little. He says he wants to investigate the reliability of the decision processes.

8

Failure Mode and Effect Analysis of Decision Processes

hen John first informs Charlotte of his intention to attempt reliability analysis of decision processes, she is confused. She thinks
that reliability is something that has to do strictly with failure of
machines or machine components. She asks him what he means by the reliability of decision processes. He begins by defining statistical reliability
(Henley and Kumamoto 1981) as the probability that a system will be func-
tioning at a specified elapsed time. The definition of a system often is taken
to mean a machine or machine component, but sometimes it is extended to
a whole set of machines. And it is not hard to see how it might also apply to
a process. Most processes, with decision processes being no exception, have
a range of behavior that can, for reliability purposes, be classified as functional or nonfunctional. This is not very different from the case of machines
or products in which failure does not mean catastrophic failure but merely
inability to meet customer expectations.

Given a classification of the process behavior as functional or nonfunctional, he says, it becomes quite natural to consider its probability of
survival.

"But," Charlotte interrupts, "a particular decision can be failed from
your way of thinking but can become acceptable at a later stage. Isn't that
fundamentally different from a machine component that stays nonfunctional once it fails?"

John considers this. "Yes," he says, "it is different to some degree, but
this difference does not eliminate the opportunity to benefit from this application of reliability techniques to our decision processes."

"The secret is to drill a little deeper into what is meant by the reliability of a component," he says. "Consider a component, say a microchip in
one of those new thermoregulators that we purchased for line 1 last year.
The manufacturer quoted a reliability of 97% under specified operational

conditions and operating intensities. But the component, the circuit board, that is physically inside the regulator in front of us will either fail or not. The reliability must refer to a population of similar components. This reliability must refer to the gross behavior of this whole population. The same is true of the decision process. For the decision process the individual decisions are the equivalent of the thermoregulators. So it should be possible to measure and target a reliability that describes the population of decisions coming from that process. For example, it might be true that there is a 95% probability of the decisions coming from the cutter adjustment decision process will be functional, that is they will be fit for use."

One common way in which to assess this reliability is to conduct a failure mode and effect analysis (FMEA). An FMEA (Stamatis 2003) surveys the risk associated with the possible ways that a process can fail to meet its fitness for use requirements. Risk is usually computed as a multiplication of the severity of the result of a failure times the probability of its occurrence. Often a third measure of detection of failure is included in the multiplication as well. Ideally, one would estimate all these inputs from data collected from the process under consideration, but often, expert opinion-based estimates are used out of necessity. The procedure can work well, but may require special considerations for rare or catastrophic events.

Charlotte is convinced that there just might something in what John is saying concerning the reliability of decision processes, so the two of them decide to reexamine the cutter adjustment decision process in this light. They enlist the help of operators, maintenance technicians, customers, and suppliers. This team receives some introduction to FMEA and proceeds to list the possible failure modes:

1. Inadequate sample taken.

2. No sample taken.

3. Faulty weight measurement.

4. Faulty length measurement.

5. Incorrect recording of weight.

6. Incorrect recording of length.

7. Incorrect rounding applied to weight.

8. Incorrect rounding applied to length.

9. Unneeded adjustment made to process.

10. Adjustment not made to process.

Each of these events can then be evaluated for its impact and its frequency of occurrence on a scale of 1 to 10, with 1 being low. Specific

FMEA systems give specific definitions to each rating level. The product of the two evaluations is taken to be the risk for each event and actions are required for high risk, which is defined here as being greater than a threshold of 80.

Table 8.1 shows a complete set of such evaluations. In this case, events that have a risk entry above 80 are mandatory, but the FMEA table also provides a ranking to guide additional efforts.

John studies the resulting table and the required actions derived from it. He agrees that either a faulty weight or a faulty length measurement can cause the decision process to fail to deliver a valid recommendation for adjustment. But it is not apparent to him exactly how he can prevent these things. He asks the team members to generate some ideas on the subject. It becomes clear almost immediately that the events have not been carefully defined. Some team members have interpreted an incorrect reading as no reading at all. In other words, they interpret this condition as the fact that the scale does not work because of poor maintenance or other reasons. Other team members interpret the incorrect reading as human error involved in reading the scale but not remembering the weight long enough to enter it correctly into the system. This discussion really clears up the problem and even though the team does not want to redo the entire FMEA, it does separate the methods of prevention into two approaches.

The operators tell horror stories about situations in which the scale was not working. They call maintenance when they become aware of this situation, but there is no recourse except to wait, carry the sample to another line, or simply wait until the next sample. The team decides that a backup scale should be made available to each line. It will be positioned on a roll-around cart so that it can be pulled into service when a particular scale goes out. It will still mean a delay in getting that first weight but probably will let the

Table 8.1   FMEA evaluations for the cutter adjustment decision.

Event	Impact	Frequency	Risk	Action required?
Inadequate sample	5	1	5	No
No sample	10	1	10	No
Faulty weight	10	10	100	Yes
Faulty length	10	10	100	Yes
Incorrect weight record	5	5	25	No
Incorrect length record	5	5	25	No
Incorrect weight round	5	10	50	No
Incorrect length round	5	10	50	No
Unneeded adjustment	1	10	10	No
No adjustment	10	10	50	Yes

crew avoid any further problems during the rest of the run. John also agrees to ask the maintenance department whether the scales can be made the subject of a project to improve their availability and reliability.

The team also addresses the other side of the problem. It is discovered that each operator has to read the scale and remember it during a 20-second walk to the recording/plotting area. And to make matters worse, some operators also use this 20 seconds to scan for aspect problems. Then the recording software is built into their intranet access, so that the operator has to fill in information on two pages before he or she can enter the actual sample information on a third page. The team recommends that the software be changed so that the weight and length information can be entered first. And the data input station is moved closer to the scale stations so the operator can record as he is looking at the readout. It is also recommended that a longer-term study be developed to see if the scale readout can be automatically stored and simply displayed to the operator so he can act on the need for adjustment if necessary.

John does not need the team to help him correct the last of the required fixes. He decides that this type of failure mode differs from the others. This one is more fundamentally related to the failure of the quality of the cutter adjustment decision process as a whole. And he has already begun to think and plan for the improvement of that process through the application of designed experiments methodology. So for now, at least until he can get that effort started, he will have to be content with the possible risks associated with this failure mode.

Although John is going to wait to complete the last improvement for the cutter adjustment decision process, he does not think that he and Charlotte need to hesitate any longer in addressing the line improvement decision process. The team that they enlist is given an introduction to FMEA, but quite a few of them are quite familiar with the method from other efforts in safety and guarantee systems. They dive right into creating this list of possible failure events:

1. Having poor cost information.

2. Having poor gain or benefit information.

3. Having wrong probabilities.

4. Improper review performed.

5. Unexpected loss of budget.

6. Operator attitude is unacceptable.

7. Data systems operate too poorly.

8. Time limitations cause a rushing of the decision.

This same set of experts compiles a corresponding list of estimates of the probability and the severity for each failure mode or event. They use a 10-point rating scale wherein 10 is extremely severe and of high probability. Furthermore, since most of the entries are based solely on expert opinion, they decide that they can resolve only three points on that scale, namely 1, 5 and 10. It is the same scale that being used for the cutter adjustment decision process FMEA and is based on the success found in that effort. (See Table 8.2.)

Table 8.2   FMEA array for the line improvement decision process.

Event	Impact	Frequency	Risk	Mandatory?
Poor cost info	5	10	50	No
Poor benefit info	5	10	50	No
Wrong probabilities	10	10	100	Yes
Improper review	1	5	5	No
Loss of budget	10	5	50	No
Operator attitude	10	1	10	No
Poor data systems	5	5	25	No
Rushed decision	5	5	25	No

The only event or mode that requires action according to the FMEA is the possibility of wrong probabilities. Already sensitized to the importance of these probabilities by his work on loss functions and impacts of poor decisions in this process, John is not overly surprised to see it come up once more. And even though the benefit and cost information-related failures have not have not passed the threshold for mandatory action, John wants to improve them as well. All three seem to be related to data collection systems or data analysis, so it will probably never be fully solved until the company establishes a fully integrated decision process quality management program. John knows that an enormous amount of work will have to be done before anything like that can happen. And he suspects that a great deal of that work will have to be accomplished by him if it is going to get done at all. This is a good long-range consideration to keep in mind as he returns to the task of making improvements in the specific decision processes into which he is investing so much effort now.

9

Control Charts for
Decision Processes

John feels that he is making considerable progress on his quest to introduce decision process quality management into the company. He has learned how to evaluate the impact of poor decisions via loss functions. He has learned how to correctly define his decision processes so that the analysis will be useful without being overwhelming. Furthermore, he has learned the process of computing capability and assessing the required stability and normality of a decision process. And he has evaluated the quality function deployment (QFD) array to ensure that the right resources are applied to the critical issues identified by his customers. Failure modes and effects analysis (FMEA) allowed him as well to guarantee the reliability of this decision processes.

He now has two significant tasks ahead of him. One task is to perform designed experiments to accelerate the decision process improvements begun by the work teams. Another task is to establish a control procedure for decision processes that can be used to control processes. He is familiar with the Shewhart x-bar and range charts from manufacturing applications and harbors the hope that these methods will be readily applicable to his decision processes.

The first thing he does is to review the philosophy and implementation of control charts (Grant and Leavenworth 1996). There is some controversy involved in this subject. Some proponents of the method see control charts as robust feedback tools that should be the primary tool in an improvement process aimed at bringing poor processes into shape. Other proponents, usually of a more statistical bent, focus on the strict definition of a process in statistical control (Montgomery, 2001). If one's process meets the conditions of statistical control, the standard control chart approach is acceptable, but otherwise one should adapt the methodology to fit the best statistical model of the process.

John has, in the course of his 13 years in manufacturing operations, applied statistical process control in both of these incarnations. He has found them both useful and imperfect at the same time. He sees the debate as turning more on the purpose of the use of the control chart than on the technical details. He recalls how one of the company statisticians called him a Bayesian because of this view. The statistician told him that Bayesians treated probability (Lee 1989) as a matter of available information rather than as a strict property of real processes. So when John treated his control charts differently depending on whether he had more or less information, the statistician interpreted this as a loose version of the Bayesian approach. John was intrigued by this concept, and had tried to conquer it at one time or another. The mathematics proved to be too deep for his abilities, but he still liked to think of himself as a Bayesian, and not without a little pride. So John again adopts his practical Bayesian attitude toward the application of control charts to decision processes. He will use them as problem-isolating tools when his process knowledge is weak and as strict statistical testing and control tools when his knowledge has increased sufficiently.

Regardless of the theory behind the control chart, its application is something more consistent. Basically it is a graphical display of the typical well-behaved distribution of values that can be produced by the process. It does not have tolerances displayed on it, and it usually works with averages of individual measurements. The control signal, at its simplest, is given whenever a plotted subgroup value goes outside two equally spaced control limits. Such a signal of the x-bar chart indicates a possible change in the mean of the process. A similar extreme point on the range chart signals a possible change in the variation of the process. The charts must be updated whenever the process is improved or modified so that this signal will be calibrated to actual conditions.

He knows that both of the decision processes under study show signs of instability and need improvement. Therefore his intention centers on an attempt to establish proper control charts that will first help stabilize and then improve these processes. John can see a little bit of Catch-22 in this approach. It is similar to employing a measurement device to evaluate its own performance. But he also can see that this approach should allow the identification of major problems, which can then be removed. The medium-sized problems can be identified and overcome, and so on until the process is stable and capable. He knows from experience that this bootstrapping approach is quite an effective approach for manufacturing processes, but he has no experience in applying it to decision processes.

He decides to begin with the cutter adjustment decision process. He asks Charlotte to help him review the currently available information from both the capability studies and historical data on this process. Charlotte reminds him that they found lots of problems with the historical data when they tried to use them as the basis for their capability study. Instead, they have chosen a more difficult approach: a special study based on differences (deltas) between the operator-recorded values and a set of expert values. Which set of data did he think was more suitable for his purpose of building control charts?

John, who had forgotten about these issues, faces a dilemma. If he uses the raw data as collected in the current data entry system, there will be problems and inconsistencies; that is, it is unstable. If he collects new samples and replicates the operator's results with those of an expert, this would give him a stable process but it will be much harder to maintain. He finally decides to try his luck with the historical data, but with the modification that he will focus on the final disposition of the sample. He will ignore the intermediate samples that can occur in the more complete process. That is, his control chart will track the ultimate decision for rejection or acceptance of a production run. This will simplify the definition of subgroups since the number of samples per run is variable. It will also emphasize the costly part of the decision process. Because he has chosen to not use an expert, his control chart can be used only to check for consistency of the decision process, but this seems agreeable enough to John. He is content with his plan.

Charlotte is assigned to collect the data from the computer systems, since she is far better at this task than John is. But, almost immediately, she stops and asks him to refine what he needs. Does he want a variable coded 0 for accept and 1 for reject? Or does he want the final recorded measurement value for each decision? If he wants the recorded measurement, does he also want to standardize it for different product weight targets? And does he want her to try to screen out apparent outliers or leave them in?

John opts for a set of data that he thinks will give good feedback without too much effort and with enough responsiveness or sensitivity to problems that the feedback will be meaningful. This means he needs a variable measurement or else he will have to wait many months to get enough decision results to see changes. It also means he wants Charlotte to do her best with the outliers, but to be conservative in her first shot and not screen too much. And, yes, he wants her to use the results across product types and even across lines, so some kind of standardization will be necessary.

Charlotte is quite capable of supplying the kind of data that John needs. The final values turn out to be 100 final weights as recorded in the current data system. She screens out about 2% of the full data as outliers but keeps the data in case they want to add it back into the dataset. And she standardizes the values for average and standard deviation of each product type over the period of a year. Figure 9.1 shows the histogram and the summary statistics that Charlotte delivers to John for use in establishing a useful control chart for the cutter adjustment decision process.

Figure 9.2 plots the data in time order, with some observations deleted because they are determined to be outliers.

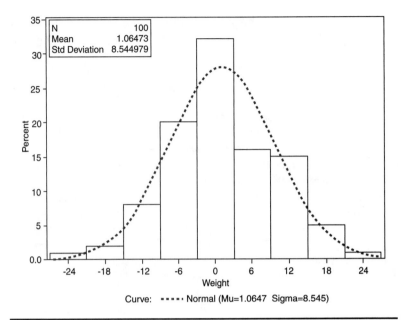

Figure 9.1   Preliminary histogram of the cutter adjustment process.

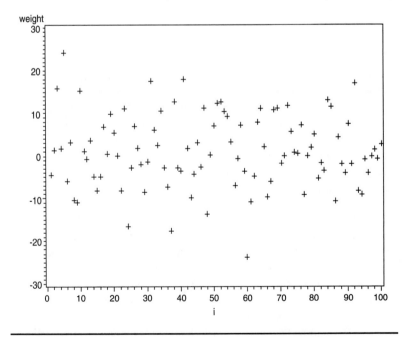

Figure 9.2   Preliminary run chart of the cutter adjustment process.

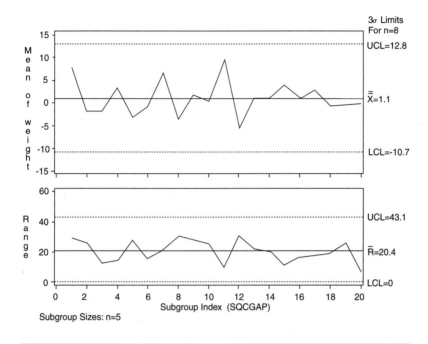

Figure 9.3   The preliminary control charts for the cutter adjustment process.

John had heard that individual charts were not highly recommended and he thinks that that there is a natural subgrouping of the values by day, which corresponds to roughly five observations. This is not true in the purest sense, since the number of runs per day varies depending on run length. But since this data is already altered by the removal of the outliers he feels the spirit of the analysis is still intact. So he uses a statistical package to compute the proper centerline and control limits for constant subgroups of size five based on this set of 100 cleansed data points. Figure 9.3 shows the data plotted against those computed control limits.

Charlotte chose her data from an older period that does not include data from the previous two months. She did this in order to see how the control charts would perform on new data that is not used in the calculation of the control limits. Figure 9.4 shows these new weights grouped by fives and plotted versus the new limits.

Both John and Charlotte are pleased with this indication that their new control limits are likely to work well when they are applied in this decision process.

John and Charlotte decide to keep this control chart themselves and share the results with the operators and technicians regularly. Although it is

weight

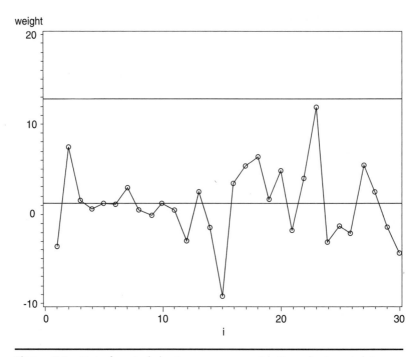

Figure 9.4 Test of control chart on more current cutter adjustment data.

often recommended that much of the value of a control chart lies in its potential for immediate feedback to the operators, they reason that since the pace of this chart is so leisurely it might work out better in this other way. They set up a simple software system to collect and update the chart and present it weekly to the crew of operators. It seems to work so well that the two of them move on to the process improvement decision process.

John contacts the company's administration department and looks into the available records of decisions related to process improvements. This creates a problem. There are records of expenditures, of course, but it is not easy to categorize and separate out the process improvement activities from other types. And these records capture only the process improvements that are funded. The process improvements that are not accepted are not tracked in any system. In the decision process capability study, John and Charlotte created artificial scenarios in order to track enough observations to get a valid estimate. They can use this method again, but it will take the extra effort of creating and presenting scenarios. And John hopes he can track the entire line management team, not just his personal results.

He and Charlotte decide that only reasonable way to go is to bite the bullet and generate a set of scenarios once a month and present them to all

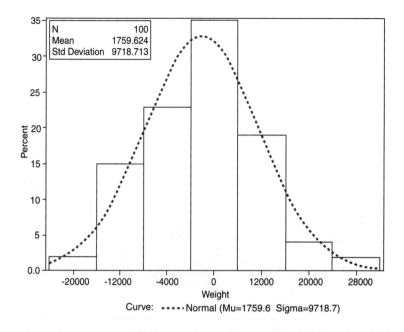

Figure 9.5   Preliminary histogram of line improvement decision process.

six line managers. This will form the logical subgroup, and they will be able to track the whole process improvement decision process. John and Charlotte do not think that they can ask all the managers to go back through the capability scenarios, so they start by using the results that John himself had generated. They also decide to use the expert solution to the problem as a correct answer so they can track stability and the degree to which the process is on target. They will use the difference between the expected gain and the estimated gain, and hence the target will be zero. They hope that any differences between the managers might wash out by using these differences in place of raw scores.

Figure 9.5 is a histogram showing the distribution of 100 of these differences after some of the abnormal values are removed.

Figure 9.6 plots the data clustered in subgroups of five, showing the control chart that is generated.

This variation is probably be a little tighter than what would be representative of all five managers, but John and Charlotte consider this a rough cut and want it to be a guide to major process problems. They expect to have to upgrade the limits once they generate new data. The actual data from the first five weeks of application of the system show a variation this is indeed larger than the baseline data. But overall the baseline is not a bad match.

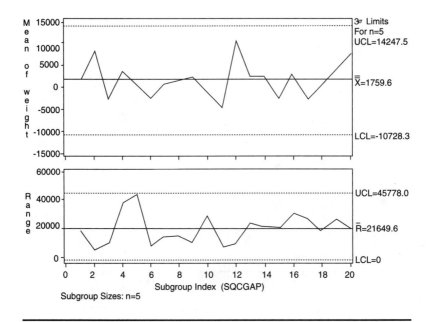

Figure 9.6 Preliminary control charts for line improvement decision process.

There are some systematic patterns in the data, but John and Charlotte decide to let the process run unless they see a clear indication of a problem. As it turns out no such problem occurs until the 16th week of using the chart. At this week the plotted point makes a step change. They track the effect to a change in the way the expert solution is computed. They readjust the centerline and continue to apply the chart.

With the control charts now implemented on the two decision processes, John and Charlotte have some confidence that they will maintain their current performance. They also plan to monitor the charts and organize some work teams with the operators to make improvements as necessary. This could be a slow process, however, and they would like to accelerate it. They have both succeeded with designed experiments on some of their previous operations studies, and they are really hopeful about applying this powerful methodology to their decision processes.

10

Decision Process Improvement via Designed Experiments

John knows that it is not unusual to find that a first capability study shows instability in a process. And he knows that it often takes quite a bit of work to get from instability to a truly capable process. Typically one must first determine whether the major problem is with the centering of the process or with its dispersion. Then one usually tries a small adjustment and recomputes the capability to see whether it is better. Then there is another small modification and another in an iterative process that can last a long time. He would like to move more quickly, in order to not lose any of the momentum that he and Charlotte have acquired. John knows that the application of designed experiments (Montgomery 2000) is especially good at just this kind of task. They are often described as one of quickest ways that an investigator can turn raw data into useful knowledge. John thinks of designed experiments as computer-aided experience. They sound perfect for his need.

The design of an appropriate experiment to study improvements of a decision process has two major parts, the soft design of experiments (DOE) piece and the hard DOE piece. The soft DOE facilitates the transformation of process expertise into the practical, implementable set of modifications that are to be made. The hard DOE shows how one can apply these modifications in a scientific way to yield hard facts about the expected performance of the decision processes once these modifications are implemented.

Soft DOE technology, like soft operations research, forms the front end of an application of the powerful technique of designed experiment technology to a decision process improvement activity. Soft DOE has the steps of:

1. Eliciting information from a team.

2. Capturing this information.

3. Using feedback to sharpen and focus the team.

4. Arriving at a strategy for the overall task.

5. Selecting an initial set of factors for study.

6. Setting levels and ranges for these factors.

7. Choosing a class of models for consideration.

8. Establishing responses and objectives for the study.

9. Reaching consensus or acceptance of the DOE setup.

10. Communicating the study to affected parties.

Many good techniques (Finegan 1998) can be applied to each of these steps. The choices should depend on the team's background and the training and consulting available to the team. John decides to focus on one particular path that he thinks will work for his process. This set of methods is generally a good one for almost any type of decision process problem, but other methods may be just as satisfactory.

In preparation John considers again the cutter adjustment decision process in which the operator takes a series of samples of extruded, cut-to-size plastic items and weighs them one by one. Based on the first weight, the operator can conclude whether the process is off target and whether a second sample weight should be taken. In this way it can be decided whether the entire production run should be scrapped or delivered to the customer. Of course, if the product is really nonconforming to specifications, the customer may reject it and the producer may be charged for the material and incur a penalty as well.

This process initially shows signs of instability and incapability. So Maxwell, the quality technician, is assigned to form a study team that will seek to improve the capability of this process. Maxwell, having extensive training and experience in non-decision process quality management, knows that a designed experiment is probably the most efficient way to approach this activity.

Maxwell assembles a study team consisting of some of the operators involved in the process, the chain supervisor, the maintenance person responsible for the cutter, the plant statistician, and himself. He explains the problem and gives a 30-minute refresher course on the virtues of designed experiments. Since most of the team is involved in the application of designed experiments to other problems, they already have a great deal of confidence in the technology and in Maxwell's ability to lead them through it.

Maxwell spends an additional hour describing the concept of decision processes to the team. He feels this is necessary, since this is the first time the team has been exposed to it. Maxwell's analogy of the decision process as a manufacturing process seems acceptable to the group. They are instructed then to focus on the decision process at hand, namely the cutter adjustment process.

The concept map is used to focus and direct the group's brainstorming activity. First a rough schematic of the decision process is drawn and displayed for the group. Each member of the group then is allowed to ask a clarifying question about the schematic or add to it. In this way a complete and well-understood map of the decision process is created.

The group is asked to create a set of responses that can be measured for this process. The fact that it is a decision process provokes questions about mind reading and crystal balls, but Maxwell keeps them on track by again using the analogy of an attribute measurement. Two responses are selected:

1. The difference between the decision made by the operator and an expert for each decision point; that is, each weight sample

2. The difference between the decision made by the operator and an expert for each run; that is, each decision to reject or accept the run.

Since no one trusts the historical data or the current data collection system, it is decided that the data should be specially collected and recorded for this experiment by members of the team. The statistician warns them that this kind of attribute measurement can require hundreds of samples to get good estimates of the factor effects and that, if at all possible, they should try to rig up a quantitative measurement. So the team rethinks the issue and comes up with these responses to replace the original ones:

1. The signed difference between the weight that the operator used to make his or her decision versus that made by the expert

2. The number of samples taken by the operator versus the number that would be taken by the expert

The collection of these responses necessitates a change to the normal procedure, but otherwise it is not difficult to accommodate the statistical needs for adequate sample size. The team agrees that these responses will be the ones they collect.

Now it is on to the selection of factors to be studied for their possible effects on improving the decision process. The team makes an initial list of 20 possible factors but whittles these down to five. This is possible because most of the 20 items such as contamination of sample and cutter breakdown are special causes that will likely cause deterioration in the performance of the decision but are unlikely to improve a decision process that is considered stable. Two of the initially suggested factors are impractical as they involve changing the product design so it will fit more easily on the scale, and one involves extensive cutter renovation. The final list of five factors is:

1. Number of weighings for each sample

2. Rounding rule

3. Time of shift

4. Operator training

5. Day of week

Even though the members know the list does not cover all the events that could occur, it is agreed that the team has a good chance to be successful. It is decided that a follow-up study might be necessary if this one does not pan out, and a secondary list is readied just in case.

Based on the recommendations of Maxwell and the statistician, the team decides to use only two settings for each of the factors since they consider this an exploratory study. They plan to follow up with full capability studies on the best-recommendation process settings delivered by the designed experiment. The statistician further educates them on the danger of missed interactions and leads them through a consideration of which interactions, if any, to consider. It is clear that this concept is not well understood by the team, and it ends with Maxwell choosing no interactions to consider. Additionally Maxwell leads the team through a selection of each of the two settings for the five factors that can be used in the shop experiment. The team thinks that the current conditions should be represented as one of the runs of the study, and Maxwell agrees to this. After reviewing the setup for the designed experiment, the shop manager asks if they can include his recommended setting; doing this would not affect the quality or efficiency of the study, so the team agrees to this request.

The final design is written by Maxwell and checked by the statistician. It is presented back to the team and to other stakeholders, including the shop manager, the quality manager, and the engineering manager. Each experimental combination will be replicated 10 times for a total of 80 production runs. This will produce at least 80 measurements on each response, but it is likely there will be around 100 if any supplemental measurements are done. Table 10.1 shows the final design agreed to by all the interested parties.

The team members are assigned to tasks such as recording the results and setting up "cheat sheets" to remind all the participants of the next trial. There are a few glitches but no loss of data, and only a small amount of production is lost because of the study. The data are checked for correctness and then collated by Maxwell, who is assigned to do the analysis with an offer of assistance from the statistician.

Maxwell is quite capable in the analysis of variance technique typically used for this type of designed experiment. He presents the result back to the team in a table and a graph, however, not in the usual analysis of variance

Table 10.1 The design array for the cutter adjustment decision process.

Combination	Weighings	Rounding	Shift time	Training	Day
1	One	1 decimal	Beginning	Basic	Monday
2	One	1 decimal	End	Advanced	Friday
3	One	3 decimals	Beginning	Advanced	Friday
4	One	3 decimals	End	Basic	Monday
5	Two	1 decimal	Beginning	Basic	Friday
6	Two	1 decimal	End	Advanced	Monday
7	Two	3 decimals	Beginning	Advanced	Monday
8	Two	3 decimals	End	Basic	Friday

table. All results are signed differences between the operator weight value and the expert weight value the team chooses as its preferred response. Table 10.2 shows the results (for the delta weight response) that Maxwell presents to the team.

Table 10.2 The results of the cutter adjustment decision process designed experiment.

		Predicted from analysis		
Factor	Significant?	Setting	Mean	Standard deviation
Rounding	Yes	One decimal	−0.15	0.16
		Three decimals	0.05	0.15
Weighings	Yes	Once	−0.07	0.22
		Two	−0.03	0.12
Training	Yes	Basic	−0.04	0.20
		Advanced	−0.06	0.14

The other two factors do not result in significant effects. Then Maxwell uses these results to select some best possible settings for the cutter adjustment decision process. He presents the top three to the team in a graphical format so the team can more fully appreciate what the numbers might mean for the actual process. Those results appear in Figure 10.1.

The team opts to try the compromise position, which does not require doubling the number of weighings, since that would potentially alter the number of samples that can be taken in a production run. The team members present their recommendations to the management team, which decides to implement them.

This is accomplished, and a new decision process capability study indicates that the process is now more capable with a C_p indicator of 1.42 and a C_{pk} of 1.28. The team is honored with an award by plant manage-

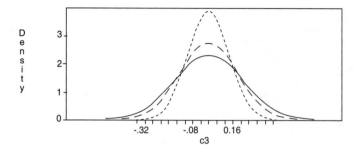

What the lines represent:
Dotted—the best setting at three-decimal rounding, two weighings, and advanced training.

Dashed—slightly cheaper at three-decimal rounding and advanced training.
Solid—cheaper still at 3 decimal rounding.

Figure 10.1 Displays of the DOE result on the cutter adjustment process.

ment. Maxwell typically gets his greatest reward from doing a job well, but he certainly does not complain about the bonus he receives for his leadership.

THE IMPROVEMENT PROJECT EXAMPLE

The shop manager, who is part of the steering committee for Maxwell's team's presentation, is encouraged by what he sees. He asks Victoria, the quality manager, to help him run a similar designed experiment on his own process improvement decision process. Victoria agrees to do this, but since she is not overly familiar with the details of designed experiments she asks Maxwell to participate as an expert consultant. He is happy to do this once his workload is adjusted so he can devote the necessary time to it. Maxwell and Victoria have some one-on-one sessions so that she can come up to speed quickly.

They assemble a team consisting of themselves, the shop manager, the managers of two other shops in the plant, and some financial and information services representatives. The financial team member has never before been asked to participate on a team and is very pleased. He needs a little extra training on the background, but his unique viewpoint proves to be quite valuable during the discussions. The problem is presented to the team, and background training brings everyone up to a working-knowledge level.

The choice of response is trickier for this problem than for the cutter adjustment decision process. This shop manager has made only 20 or so historical decisions of this nature. After lengthy discussions in which the team members struggle to get their heads around this situation, they decide they can use the decision scenario approach that was successfully applied to the decision capability study. It is decided that they will use the difference between the projected gain for each decision that the shop manager made on each decision scenario versus the best outcome that can be generated by the detailed expert approach.

To determine which factors to use, the team revisits some of the brainstorming done for the capability study and decides to build its list of factors for the designed experiment on that original list. Half the team members think this list is sufficient, but the others want two more factors added. Since the designed experiment can hold up to seven factors without additional trials, the team decides to keep both sets of factors in the study. Because of this compromise the experiment is a little harder to perform, but the whole team can support the results because all interests are covered. The seven factors are:

1. Time of budget

2. Amount of request

3. Requestor expertise

4. Type of improvement

5. Formality of request

6. Cost reduction programs

7. Project accounting report format

With the help of the statistician they conclude that a minimum of eight pseudo-replicates will have to be created for each combination in the designed experiment array. Since Victoria has spent some time already with scenario creation and because the information services representative can automate the process of creating the scenarios, the team recommends 10 scenarios for each trial if the manager and the expert can schedule the time.

The team does not spend too much time on the selection of levels for each of the factors. They readily agree that two settings for each will be a good place to start, and many of those settings are considered obvious. Only the last two factors introduced by the financial representative need any detailed consideration, simply because members are unfamiliar with them. After a satisfactory explanation the team readily agrees to these settings as well. Despite warnings from the statistician about hidden interactions, the team feels that it can ignore these without compromising the study too much.

The proposed designed experiment conditions are reviewed by the steering committee and agreed to by the shop manager. He hoped that they could simply reuse the scenarios that had been generated in the capability study, but he is finally convinced that all new ones must be run because of the two new factors that are added. This effort will add another 20 hours to his workload over the next four weeks but he is used to long hours; if this could improve his decisions he is willing to contribute the time. Table 10.3 shows the finalized designed experiment conditions; factors 1 through 7 are abbreviated in order to reduce the clutter of the array.

Table 10.3   The design array for the process improvement decision process.

Scenario	Date	Amount	Expertise	Type	Formality	Reductions	Report
1	Early	<$1000	Low	Hard	Formal	Yes	Old
2	Early	<$1000	High	Soft	Formal	No	New
3	Early	>$1000	Low	Hard	Informal	Yes	New
4	Early	>$1000	High	Soft	Informal	No	Old
5	Late	<$1000	Low	Hard	Informal	No	New
6	Late	<$1000	High	Soft	Informal	Yes	Old
7	Late	>$1000	Low	Hard	Formal	No	Old
8	Late	>$1000	High	Soft	Formal	Yes	New

Ten scenarios are considered replicates in that the expected value of the best decision is equivalent irrespective of different words being used in the problem description. While they are constructing these replicate scenarios, Maxwell notices that, if done correctly, the scenarios could be used to study the robustness of the decision in the same way that robust engineering methods work. He jots this idea down as something he would like to explore later. The scenarios are updated to include the two new factors and are presented to the shop manager in small batches. All eight scenario types are presented two times in a session in a randomized order, and there are five sessions spaced over a four-week period. The results are collected automatically through the software that information services created and then exported to a file that Maxwell and Victoria can use to complete the analysis.

Again Maxwell and Victoria use the analysis of variance technique that is recommended for the designed experiment approach but translate their findings into a form more palatable for the presentation. The response is the difference in dollars between the shop manager's decision and the expert decision. Because this is the first application of decision process analysis of this type performed at the company, the presentation is well attended by both plant personnel and corporate staff. Even the vice president of the division is there. Table 10.4 contains the results as presented by Victoria with strong support from Maxwell.

Then in graphical format they present the proposed modifications that produce the best improvement versus the current situation (Figure 10.2).

Table 10.4   The results from the process improvement decision process designed experiment.

Factor	Significant?	Predicted from analysis		Standard deviation
		Setting	Mean	
Expertise	Yes	Low	$1000	$2500
		High	$1100	$1500
Type	Yes	Hard	$550	$1750
		Soft	$1550	$1750
Report	Yes	Old	$1250	$1700
	No	New	$750	$1800

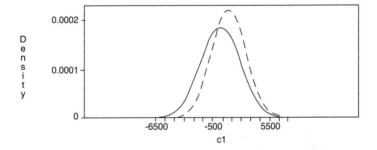

Solid line—the results of an average of all current conditions.	**Dotted line**—the expected impact under the setting of expertise = high, type = hard, and report = new.

Figure 10.2   Display of the DOE results on the line improvement decision process.

These differences represent the gaps between the shop manager's decisions and the best decisions based on available information. That is, these are biases built into his decision process. The improvement is to educate the shop manager so that he no longer has these biases. He agrees to pay more attention to this effect and to review his performance more frequently. The third factor can be changed simply by getting rid of the old accounting report formats more quickly. This is in concert with what the financial department wants anyway, so that department is happy to spearhead this effort.

The success of this project strikes a chord with the corporate staff members. They decide to start a comprehensive corporate program to examine the major decision processes of the company. And since the shop manager John is now considered the expert, he is appointed to head this effort with an accompanying raise and promotion. He asks that Charlotte, Victoria, and

Maxwell be appointed to a special support team for this effort answering directly to him. Victoria turns the opportunity down since she has other career plans, and Charlotte is instead asked to take over John's shop manager job; she gleefully accepts. John and Maxwell turn to their next challenge: turning their early successes into an unending string of new successes.

11

Algorithmic Statistical Process Control for Decision Processes

John, the shop manager, now occupies a corporate position with the objective of bringing decision process management more generally to the company. But he does not know immediately where to start. He has only applied quality management to two decision processes so far and has no idea whether the same approach will be successful in other situations. So he does what has brought him to his current position: he wings it and talks to the experts. First he talks at length to Maxwell, the statistician. Maxwell advises him that the same methods could work for most decision processes, but some adaptation might be necessary. Maxwell, who is good at solving problems, advises John to identify some worthy problems and just give it a go.

So John begins a survey of decision processes scattered throughout the business. He is amazed to see how many decisions are made daily, and how many of these decisions seem to be patches or reworks of previous decisions that have gone sour. He is also amazed that no one seems to be paying any attention to these decisions. Managers appear to assume that since humans are making the decisions, they can't be improved upon. Everybody seems to shrug their shoulders and say that decisions cannot be studied; they must simply be accepted as the best that anyone can do in the particular situation. This tendency to avoid questioning the adequacy of decisions is especially prevalent in management at all levels of the company hierarchy.

John concludes from this survey that decision processes are a likely blind spot for his company. He sees the fundamental challenge of his new position to be exposing this blind spot. He gathers his survey of decision processes and brainstorms over them one long night with Maxwell and Victoria. They decide to choose two decision processes on which to work. These decision processes should be visible to upper management but not be of a critical nature to company survival. They want to find processes to which the techniques of quality management will be readily adaptable as well. And they also want their processes to be in areas that will help them learn about the use of applying these methods all across the company.

None of the processes that are on their initial list fits all three criteria exactly, but some seem very close. One of these is a decision process used by the research and development personnel to qualify new products. Another suitable decision process concerns the kinds of research that are done on marketing their products to potential customers. Both of these processes have been identified as inadequate by company management and already have some resources commissioned for study teams. John hopes that he will be able to piggyback on some of this work to further the decision process management objectives that he is promoting. The next day John contacts the research and development team and assigns Maxwell to contact the marketing team.

John is acquainted with the team leader for the research and development improvement team. The leader, Carly, holds a Ph.D. in chemistry. She believes strongly that chemistry has all the answers, and any quality problems must be due to the inability of the manufacturing sites to make the product as it was designed. It clearly could not be a problem with the design. She explains to John that the current efforts of the team are focused on categorizing the product qualifications that have been made over the past five years by product type, market, and development time. This is almost ready. When it is ready, she is going to have a set of her chemists review it with an eye to seeing if something comes to them as to ways to improve the process.

John asks her whether it might be a good idea to have people outside of the group share this review, and she does not see the necessity of this action, since it is the designers who know the most about the issues. John also asks if Carly is going to collect some other information like manufacturing costs and quality costs related to the products, but again her viewpoint is that her department's job is to design the best product it can, and it is manufacturing's job to figure out how to produce it correctly. John asks to be included in the discussions; Carly reluctantly agrees because John's project has high-level corporate backing.

John schedules meetings over the next three weeks with anyone who has knowledge or interest in this process for choosing new product designs. He also diagrams the process for himself and identifies the inputs and outputs to the decision. He focuses on the decision process that is to be used on the next set of decisions at the quarterly design review.

The process as he identifies it is the following:

The design team consists of Carly and 3 chemist/designers selected on a rotating basis from a staff of 14 such scientists. The head of marketing and the head of research and development are always invited to attend but seldom do. They are required to make one of three decisions on each proposed new product: thumbs-up, thumbs-down, or table for one quarter while awaiting more complete information. The inputs they use to make this decision for each proposed product consist of a written prospectus that contains an estimate of sales volume over three years, an estimate of development cost, and product portfolio rating indicating how well it fit into the current product mix. The decision team then discusses the merits of the proposal and makes the decision. Rejected proposals can be reintroduced with new elements six months or more after rejection.

Using the inputs that he received from around the company, John constructs a list of factors that can affect the decision quality. As he peruses the list he is happy to see that many of the items are similar to those on the list he made for his own decision process not long ago. Perhaps it will not be that hard to use the same methods on new processes after all. Here is John's new list:

1. Size of sales volume

2. Size of development cost

3. Time of budget year

4. Presence or absence of nonchemists

5. Previous number of attempts rejected

6. Expertise of submitter

7. Completeness of proposal

8. Originality of proposed product

John can already see how a well-designed experiment can be used to try out some modifications efficiently. To apply his previous methods to the new process, all he needs is a good set of responses and a way to measure them.

Enlisting the experts again, John and the team, which includes Maxwell, decide they want most to have the decision process consistent. Finding some improvements that will allow less variation would be the best outcome. John thinks they can probably find a way to be more accurate also, but he accommodates others' wishes and targets decision process variation reduction as the primary concern. They will generate replicate scenarios based on modifications of actual situations. These modifications will be based on the designed experiment array, and the team will group the replicates from each test condition into subsets and compute their standard deviations. These standard deviations will serve as the basis for analysis. A rating of each proposal will make on scale of 1–10 to get better resolution than the original three-point system. They meet three times over the course of two weeks and design the experiment shown in Table 11.1.

Table 11.1   The design array for the new product design process.

Condition	Sales	Cost	Time	Chemists	Rejects	Expert	Original
1	>$500K	>$50K	Early	Only	0	Yes	Yes
2	>$500K	>$50K	Late	Others	0	No	No
3	>$500K	<$50K	Early	Others	>0	No	No
4	>$500K	<$50K	Late	Only	>0	Yes	Yes
5	<$500K	>$50K	Early	Only	>0	No	Yes
6	<$500K	>$50K	Late	Others	>0	Yes	No
7	<$500K	<$50K	Early	Only	0	Yes	No
8	<$500K	<$50K	Late	Others	0	No	Yes

John leads his study team in a presentation of this proposed designed experiment to the R&D staff, some of the corporate staff, and Carly and her chemistry team. Most of the attendees accept the approach and see no real issues in whatever conclusions it might generate. The marketing manager, however, raises an issue. Most of the factors make sense to him, but the one on projected sales seems to be not a useful factor. They can't control it to any extent, even though his organization is committed to tweaking it as much as possible. Even if the experiment shows that this is the dominant factor, it is more of an input that they must adjust for rather than a factor that they can directly control. The rest of the proposal is okay, he says, but they need to do something else about the effect of sales.

John and his team go back to the drawing board. They know that the marketing manager is right. When a decision is made, the process has to be adjusted for the effect of the sales number. In fact, as the team considers this issue they decide that it is really the ratio of sales to cost that is the driver. It can, and probably should, affect the decision process. It should be adjusted out in the process, but this adjustment has to be contemporaneous with the decision itself because the economic conditions can change quarterly. The remaining question is how to work this adjustment into the decision process improvement effort.

Maxwell again comes to John's rescue, suggesting that the team apply a variation of algorithmic statistical process control (ASPC) (Vander Wiel et al. 1992) to the problem. ASPC, Maxwell explains, is a synthesis of the standard quality management techniques that has grown out of statistical process control and the method of engineering control wherein compensations to the process are made by feedback loops. For example, Maxwell says, the process modification that started all these studies—the one that Charlotte originally suggested to John—is an example of a feedback system. This particular feedback system will involve the automatic weighing of sample products periodically during a production run. Then the deviation from target of the current sample, plus the history of previous adjustments, can be used to automatically feed back a new pressure setting for the extruder vault. In this way any variations in feedstock or line speed can be compensated for by the pressure adjustments.

John understands this concept, for it had been covered in a university engineering course that he had taken toward his degree. In fact, he had always found this approach to make more sense to him than the quality management approach as embodied in a control chart with action rules and process interruptions. "Yes," he says, "I understand the automatic feedback part, but how does this interface with the SPC or TQM piece to form this ASPC thing?"

"Well," Maxwell answers, "the feedback system can do a great job of compensating for expected variations in a decision process, but it never really leads to fundamental improvement of the process by itself. And there are some disturbances such as breakdowns or operator effects that it cannot effectively compensate. But if you can use both the automatic approach and the TQM approach, you can deal with both types of issues and do a lot better job. The trick is to assume that the automatic adjustment is in place and then tune your standard analysis to accommodate this fact."

The usual application of ASPC is in control of a system. For example, one may take the errors that are left from the automatic process adjustment and examine them via Shewhart control charts for shifts or trends that exist despite the adjustment and that can be corrected more permanently. If one can make such improvements, it should improve the capability of the process and of the adjustment system as well, so it can be a win-win situation.

John says that it sounds good but how could they apply this ASPC approach to the improvement work that he is contemplating for the decision involving the new products? Maxwell tells John that it sounds as if the sales estimates are much like the uncontrollable variation that is compensated for by the automatic feedback system. And the other factors can be studied for their effects on the decision process after it has been adjusted for sales. This is in the spirit of ASPC, even if it is not a typical implementation.

So John and Maxwell explain ASPC to the team, which agrees to modify its approach to accommodate this automatic feedback explicitly. That is, the team members will offer the scenarios for each of the designed experiment conditions at several levels of the sales/cost ratio estimate. Then they will treat the response variability as curves depending on the sales/cost ratio input. They will choose the setting that reduces variability in the decisions as a function of the sales/cost ratio.

Since the team members now need to generate a set of replicate scenarios for each design array combination for several settings of price/cost ratio, they opt to reduce the number of factors by eliminating the originality factor and the factor related to the makeup of the team. Some team members argue

Table 11.2 The modified design array for the new product design process.

Ratio	Time	Rejects	Expert	Condition
Low	Early	0	Yes	1
Low	Early	>0	No	2
Low	Late	>0	Yes	3
Low	Late	0	No	4
Medium	Early	0	Yes	1
Medium	Early	>0	No	2
Medium	Late	>0	Yes	3
Medium	Late	0	No	4
High	Early	0	Yes	1
High	Early	>0	No	2
High	Late	>0	Yes	3
High	Late	0	No	4

that this effect is accounted for by the portfolio fit rating anyway and that the chemists-only option is clearly a bad idea but one that has just evolved. This leaves only three factors, since cost and sales have been combined, and the array is to be replicated for each setting of this ratio. This can be handled by only four array conditions. Also it is decided that the number of runs can be reduced to eight per condition and that there will be three levels of sales/cost ratio set at low, medium, and high values. Putting everything together means that four array conditions are repeated for each of three settings of ratio with eight replicate scenarios at each one, or $4 \times 3 \times 8 = 96$ total scenarios and an equal number of decisions to be made by the review committee. Table 11.2 contains the set of conditions that are encoded into scenarios and presented to the decision-making team.

Here are the results of the analysis that John performed. He uses analysis of variance for the subsets of data for each of the sales/cost ratios that are studied. He finds his recommendations for lowest variability conditions differ quite dramatically depending on the cost/ratio value under which the decisions are determined. Table 11.3 summarizes the results that he and the study team present at the steering committee meeting.

John and Maxwell also include a two-slide graphical depiction (Figure 11.1) of a projection of what the gain will be for the best condition and the current typical condition. The first slide shows the current variation as the solid curve, the expected variation for low ratio in the dashed curve, the expected variation for the medium ratio in the dotted curve and the expected variation for the high ratio in the dash-dotted curve.

Figure 11.2 shows the comparison of the average variability for the current situation given in the solid curve and the average variability averaged

Table 11.3 The results of the new product design process designed experiment.

| Ratio value | Factor | Predicted for analysis | | Standard deviation |
		Setting	Significant?	
Low	Time	Early	Yes	2.75
		Late		1.75
Medium	Time	Early	Yes	2.95
		Late		2.55
	Rejects	0	yes	2.25
		>0		3.25
High	Expert	Yes	Yes	2.50
		No		3.50

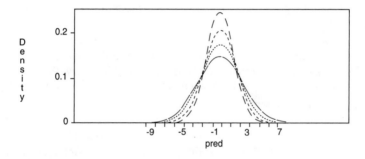

Figure 11.1 Display of the DOE on the new product selection process.

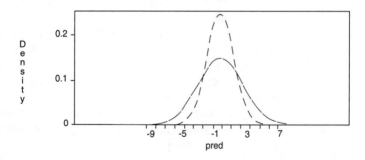

Figure 11.2 Display of ASPC-adjusted DOE results for the new product selection process.

over the three ratio levels if the decision procedure is changed in an automatic fashion when economic conditions cause a change in the sales/cost ratio.

The presentation team is justifiably proud of its efforts. The members are able to identify changes that appear to yield a 24% reduction in decision process variability. After the presentation, the steering committee agrees to implement the findings and track the results. Upon implementation these turn out as expected, achieving a 40% reduction versus the historical average. This gain depends on the fact that the current economic conditions are poor and are keeping the sales/cost ratio low. But managers expect some savings no matter what the ratio turns out to be.

After the meeting the senior vice president has a long conversation with John about the potential of this approach for other decision process management efforts. John says he has only anecdotal information, but based on the few sample projects he has high expectations for future efforts. John adds that the project Maxwell is working on should come to fruition soon and will add to his confidence in the methods. The senior vice president asks John to update him as soon as he has these further results. The executive is considering sponsoring wider activity in this area with more dedicated resources, and he wants John's advice on how to set up this decision process quality program.

Maxwell meets with the marketing manager and explains his task. Nermal, the marketing manager, is eager to have Maxwell's help in working on his marketing problem. It seems that the company is losing market share, and something has to be done about it as soon as possible. Nermal already has brought in an independent consultant who benchmarked their systems against some of the industry leaders, but no major improvements have been produced from this work. Nermal has read about a number of approaches to the problem, but they all seem to require boatloads of money and lots of time to take effect. Confidentially, Nermal admits that he has maybe six months to make some improvements or he might as well start job hunting.

Maxwell assures Nermal that he will try to help, but he won't guarantee that enough improvement can be accomplished quickly. Nevertheless, he can get started as soon as Nermal is ready. They form a team and call their first meeting the very next day. The team consists of Maxwell, Nermal, two account executives, and a marketing analyst. Nermal introduces Maxwell and invites him to explain the process. Maxwell does his best, but it is clear that quality management techniques have not yet penetrated into the marketing department and only the analyst has a quantitative background. In the final analysis Maxwell feels that the team will be willing to follow his lead since they have been well motivated by management. They feel just as frustrated as their manager does at the unexpected loss of market share. Maxwell decides that the best course of action is to teach by doing, so he asks them to explain the process of identifying marketing strategy to him in detail.

The process of identifying potential customers is described. The theory is that there are market segments and that each segment has a fixed purchasing capacity in units. It is deemed nearly impossible to enter a market with a new product while it is absorbing a new product, but penetration can occur if the purchasing in the segment has stabilized. The whole idea is to select the proper market timing through four fundamental steps:

1. Track the buying history of each segment.

2. Separate the history into an absorption period and a stable period.

3. Within the stable period determine a proper delay time.

4. Initiate the results are used to set pricing and marketing strategy.

Upon discussion prompted by Maxwell, the team further isolates the decision process that is the major component of step 3: identifying the beginning of the stable period.

The data set from each segment is a statistically stratified sample that an external company manages and then sells to their company. It is considered unimpeachable as a source, although there have been a few times when the company's managers felt the numbers were a little shaky. This data are prepared and summarized into charts and tables by the analyst, who presents them to the decision team. These charts are line graphs of the buying history weekly for the current period, usually three months, and then extending at least nine months prior to the current data in order to make a full year's worth of data. The team looks at the chart and will ask the analyst to drill down on certain aspects of the chart or delete specified points until the team reaches a consensus about the right separation of the buy-in from the stabilized period. The analyst sometime superimposes control limits and other statistical aids, but these are not well understood by the decision team and are not used consistently. The result of the decision is an estimate of the start of the stable period and its duration until the current date. Experience suggests that new product introduction should occur precisely six weeks after the onset of the stagnation interval. The team reviews this data monthly. A determination of stabilization initiates a sequence of events that constitutes the marketing program for the new product.

Maxwell probes into this decision delicately but deeply. He asks if there are other important inputs such as the type of product, or whether the last product was introduced by their company or by a competitor. The team members assure him that to the best of their knowledge these factors do not

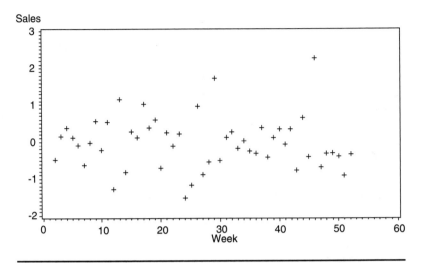

Figure 11.3   Example of the time plots for marketing decision process.

matter. They have found that only highly unusual economic conditions like a sustained national recession seem to affect this process, and they do not want to treat that eventuality. It is the marketing analyst who finally volunteers that he has, over the years, found that there is some evidence of a pattern in time. There seems to be an up-and-down cycle inherent in the decision process. That is, a long determination of the last event usually leads to a short determination in the current interval and vice versa.

Maxwell has the analyst show him examples of the data plots that he shows the decision team. Figure 11.3 shows one such plot taken from the hundreds that Maxwell is shown.

It certainly is not apparent to Maxwell at which point one can separate this plot into one or more intervals of initialization and stabilization. He realizes that he is not an expert and that he has little experience in interpreting these graphs, but he certainly suspects that there could be a lot of variation in this process.

His instinct tells him that a designed experiment might help improve the process, but the group is not able to identify any feasible factors to employ in such an experiment. It turns out to be lucky for Maxwell that just at this moment John asks him to help with the R&D product choice decision process. Perhaps it is just wishful thinking, but the ASPC concept seems to be applicable to the marketing problem. Maybe a hidden feedback or pattern in the historical series makes it more difficult to ascertain the two periods. Maybe if he does some data analysis he can figure it out without a designed experiment.

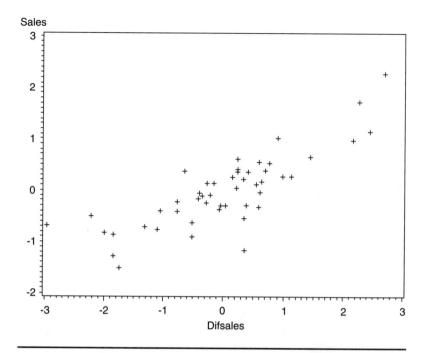

Figure 11.4 Differences in consecutive points for marketing decision process.

He tries several plots and ways of looking at the data, until he happens on something that really works well. Once he has it, he recalls the analyst's comment about the relationship between the current sales and the previous sales, and it seems to make sense. Maxwell has computed the differences between consecutive weekly data points and plots these differences against the current sales values to get the plot shown in Figure 11.4.

Maxwell uses regression to find the best fitting line to this apparent trend. The slope comes out to be around 0.5, meaning that sales go up about half as fast as the difference in sales. Maxwell reasons that if he subtracts 0.5 of last month's sales out of the current sales he may reveal more of the underlying structure, that is, the difference between the two types of sales periods that the decision team is seeking. Figure 11.5 is the graph he gets after computing these corrected sales values and plotting them against week.

When he shows this plot to the team members, they are ecstatic and immediately agree that this is a huge improvement over what they have had. The team conducts a study comparing the team's ability to detect intervals with the corrected sales versus the uncorrected and finds that the variation

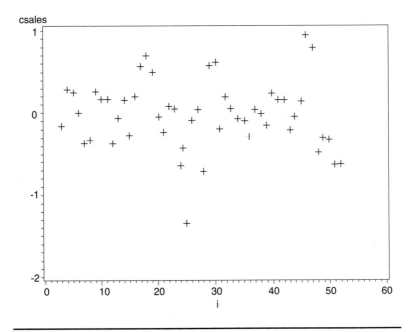

Figure 11.5 Marketing data adjusted for time pattern.

drops by 50%! The marketing manager takes the entire team out for an excellent meal to show his appreciation of their efforts.

When John hears the story of the marketing department's success, he contacts the senior vice president, and he and Maxwell present the full set of results to him. As a consequence the executive follows up on his plans and offers to appoint John and Maxwell to the task of designing and implementing a full decision process quality management program. He and Maxwell are asked to move over to offices in corporate headquarters so it will be easier to communicate with corporate staff officers. They are more than overjoyed at the success of their results and agree readily to this offer. They steal a glance at each other as if to say that they will certainly have their work cut out for them coming up with a full decision management program from scratch.

12

Implementing a Decision Process Quality Management Program

John realizes that it is one thing to string together a few successful projects, but it is a completely different challenge to develop and implement a program for the company as a whole. He still remembers his first month as a manager after being a product design engineer for two years. He expected everybody to be as excited about his appointment as he was, and it was quite a learning experience to realize that it was he who had to change and accommodate. But he learned, and he plans to build on that experience to help him with this new task.

The first thing he decides to do is check out the experts. And by experts he means the other managers who have built successful programs. He talks to the woman who has built a successful employee suggestion plan, and she suggests that he get to know upper management since they are the ones who pay the bills. Then John speaks with the man who supervised the recent downsizing that shrank the company payroll by 15%. He suggests that the most important thing to do is to create a schedule and get commitment for resources up front, and then keep a close eye on the details as the program unfolds. And John also discusses these issues with at least six other managers at his new peer level. They give him lots of good advice.

Then he hits the books. There are hundreds of books on management styles (Merli 1990), all guaranteed to bring success, and hundreds more on quality management (Garvin 1988). So John enlists Maxwell to help him read some of the more pertinent ones and synthesize the findings. They look over all the examples of success and winnow the critical actions that led to these successes. They also look at failures and try to understand how to avoid them. Then they brainstorm and get feedback and revise their plans. Only when they are convinced that they have a plan for a program that will be flexible and successful do they propose it to their sponsor, the senior vice president.

The program that John and Maxwell design consists of five primary elements. The elements are:

1. Clear communication from management of the importance of the program

2. A method to motivate employees at all levels to support the program

3. Overview training for appropriate personnel, especially line management

4. A guarantee of sufficient resources for one year until the program becomes self-supporting

5. Strong integration of the program into business process planning, including the tracking of indicators of program success

They estimate the costs of this effort and put together a projected pay-off table showing that the program has the objective of becoming a self-supporting cost center within two years of inception. Internal resources can deliver most of the training, since it will only be a minor modification of the standard quality management training. They also think that they can piggyback on several currently successful programs such as the employee suggestion system. In addition, they present a list of projected resource needs.

The vice president is quite supportive of their approach during their subsequent presentation to the entire senior staff. The CEO and most of the long-term members of the staff do not support the idea. They cannot see how decisions can be put under scientific control. But they have seen the benefits of their quality program and know that there is lots of waste and non-value-added work in the manufacturing operations, so it seems like this effort cannot cause any real harm. The problem is, of course, allocating a budget. The senior managers say that they simply do not have enough funds to follow through on all the ideas that are presented to them, no matter how good they are. Maybe if John and Maxwell come back after some more fundamental work has been finished there might be some funds available. In their minds there is a lot more work needed in other areas than tweaking the good decision processes that they have now.

John and Maxwell have expected this argument and even though they have presented evidence against this line of reasoning, they also know that they are unlikely to win this argument on logic alone. Many managers, especially top managers at this company, resort to personal instinct to make decisions. They are the least likely persons in the company to want to install decision process quality management, since it might restrict their freedom to act in their accustomed manner. In the end it is networking that saves the day. John and Maxwell are just about to accept defeat when their sponsor speaks up for them. He commits to personally overseeing the effort and pretty much guarantees a successful implementation. John and Maxwell know that he is sticking his neck out on their behalf, and they are thankful for the support. Of course, even with this commitment the other senior managers force them to accept a 20% reduction in budget and an accelerated timetable for implementation, but this is a small price to pay for the opportunity they have been afforded. John and Maxwell have their decision process quality management program for real now!

They spend the next two weeks organizing resources and coordinating with the other programs that they hope to piggyback. They help the vice president word the announcement and set the goals for the program. And they review the business plans of the each of the divisions in order to make sure their first projects are chosen in such a way as to have an substantial impact on real business needs. They also hope that they can identify some low-hanging fruit so they can get some big winners immediately.

The announcement of the program creation is made, and immediately John and Maxwell follow up with announcements of how the employees can use the employee suggestion system to bring attention to decision processes that can be evaluated. Several training sessions are also offered to employees as an overview, and detailed sessions on methodology are offered to anyone who wants to be more informed. Then John and Maxwell wait for responses.

Responses are mixed. Some ideas come quickly from individuals who are obviously motivated to make organizational changes. Some responses are mere gripes. There are whole divisions that give no feedback whatsoever. And then there are individuals who send in as many as a dozen ideas at once. About 150 individuals request the introductory training and about 100 actually show up to take it. Twenty-five individuals ask for the more detailed week-long training session, and the class size turns out to be 18. Only 15 managers voluntarily attend the overview training, and only one attends the intensive session. This is not the overwhelming reception that John and Maxwell had hoped for, but they are realistic enough to accept the situation and apply remedial action.

Although they wish for the voluntary participation of everyone, they can see that this is not going to happen. So they set up mandatory one-hour training sessions for all lower- and medium-tier management and for most of the staff. Then they have a decision process quality management, objective written into each middle- and lower-level manager's objectives. And they create a set of objectives that measure activity on this front that will be reported each month back to all management levels. These same indicators become part of the weekly updates that are given to all personnel as well.

The indicators they use to monitor the health of the decision process quality management program are threefold:

1. The number of proposals/suggestions identified per week

2. The percentage of departments that made proposals per week

3. The gains in dollars per week

John and Maxwell hope that the first indicator will show that the program is penetrating deeply into the company. The second indicator is designed to show that the program is spreading widely throughout the organization. And the third indicator measures the value of the program to basic business results. They know that in the early stages of the program the first two indicators will probably be the most valuable for keeping the program alive and growing, but they both realize that only solid performance in the last indicator will make it viable in the long term.

Figures 12.1–12.4 show the kind of results the duo distribute regularly throughout the company.

The vertical line on the gains charts shows the point at which the costs for the decision process quality management program will be paying for itself. Anything above that line shows that as a cost center John and Maxwell are making money for the company. Several other programs adopt the same approach as its success becomes evident in the company.

The decision processes of the company are documented as the projects amass. A few groups, such as legal and security, insist on remaining outside, but it becomes harder and harder over time for them to persist in their resistance. John and Maxwell do not publicize those departments' noncooperation as they think this might turn the attitude to one of belligerence, but they do continually try to involve legal and security personnel in decision process improvement work so they can get more comfortable with it. They also continue to do follow-up courses as interest continues to build over the weeks of hard work.

After the first eight months of success, John and Maxwell are asked to set up a vendor improvement program. They design this pretty much the same way they have the internal program and insist that its success also be monitored regularly by upper management and that it too pay its own way by a specific date. The program has its bumps and requires a management change halfway into it, but once it gets its act in order the savings are quite impressive and the vendors themselves come to think of it as giving them a distinct advantage over their competitors.

Maxwell and John feel overwhelmed when they start the program and work lots of hours, but the apparent ease with which they are able to get improvements constantly motivates them. Apparently the fact that decision processes have been ignored for so long means that lots of big gains are

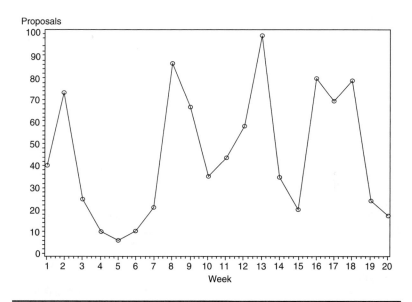

Figure 12.1   Tracking of decision process improvement proposals.

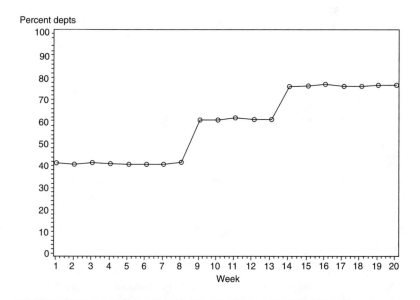

Figure 12.2   Tracking of penetration of decision process quality management.

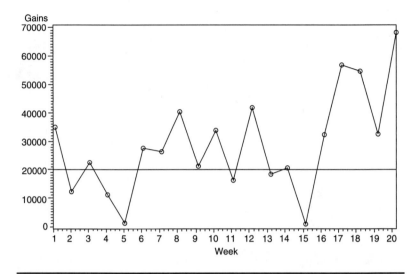

Figure 12.3 Tracking of gains from decision process quality management projects.

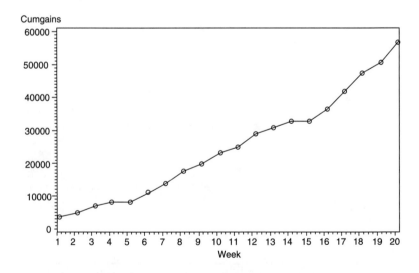

Figure 12.4 Tracking of cumulative gains from decision process quality management projects.

available through pretty simple improvements. Maxwell and John, having come from the manufacturing world in which the smallest process improvements sometimes cost a lot of time, effort, and money, are surprised but gratified to see that improvement elsewhere can be a lot easier. By the end of the first year they have exceeded their projections of gains by 150% and are self-sufficient six months ahead of schedule. When they present these results to the senior staff, there are fewer cynics since their gains are so well founded. They ask for and receive permission to expand the department by two persons. Most of the senior staff still resists applying the methodology at their level, but a few inroads are paved. For example, the CEO asks all the senior staff to attend the one-hour introductory session for information's sake. The CEO further asks that all departments try to initiate some projects this year, in order to bring the percentage of involved departments to 100%. This is welcome news to John and Maxwell, who have consistently failed to get the interest of some holdout departments. Maybe in this way they can get better cooperation in those neglected areas and fully penetrate all divisions of the organization.

They know that they have to get back to work and continue to grow and improve their program. It does not matter how successful they have been so far if they cannot sustain progress over the long haul. One thing that they work hard at establishing in the second year of the program is a decision process knowledge warehouse (Lee and Strong 2003), which is used to capture important aspects of the processes and their improvements so the knowledge can be readily accessed and used by those who need to know in the organization.

They also undertake a critical review of the program and make adjustments as need be. One change they make is to more closely align their project cost accounting to the business financial definitions and procedures. Another change is the incorporation of new software to generate the decision process scenarios that are so often used in the capability and improvement work. They also start to work with some of the more difficult problems and, although this slows down their results, the size of eventual gains more than compensates for the delay. But they run the program as a cost center and always make sure that they meet their financial obligations to senior management. By the end of the second year they have 96% participation and have gains that consistently pass $250,000 per month.

After the program has been running successfully for four years, a management change in the senior staff helps their cause even further. The CEO has decided to retire and the senior vice president who sponsors them is on the short list to replace her. It is partially because of the success of the decision process quality management program that this vice president is finally appointed to that high position by the company's board of directors. They like the results that he has achieved over the years by relying on data and facts to make his decisions. They see that the company will be facing some extremely tough situations in the near future due to some government regulation changes and the expansion of an Asian competitor into the market, and they think that this kind of leadership is going to turn out to be critical for the company.

Not long after the announcement of the management change, John and Maxwell are informed that the new CEO would like to see them. Over a fine dinner, the three of them talk for a long time of the successes of the program and how it is instrumental to their own success. The meeting ends with a substantial raise for John and Maxwell, and a request by the CEO that they extend their decision process quality management program to the senior staff as well, including him. He warns them that they still will have their detractors and that his support alone will not always carry the day, but it should be a lot easier to push the program to the last corners of the organization now and improve some of the decisions made at the highest levels of this concern. In fact, he would like them to start on several problem areas as soon as they can. Maxwell and John know that another challenge is just beginning for them!

Bibliography

Automobile Industry Action Group (AIAG). *Measurement Systems Analysis,* 3rd ed. DaimlerChrysler, Ford Motor, and General Motors, 2002.

Berk, Joseph, and Susan Berk. *Total Quality Management.* New York: Sterling Publishing, 1993.

Besterfield, Dale H. *Quality Control,* 6th ed. Columbus, OH: Prentice Hall, 2001.

Campanella, Jack, Ed. *Principles of Quality Costs: Principles, Implementation, and Use,* 3rd ed. Milwaukee: ASQ Quality Press, 1999.

Casti, John L. *Alternate Realities.* New York: John Wiley and Sons, 1989.

English, Larry P. *Improving Data Warehouse and Business Information Quality: Methods for Reducing Costs and Increasing Profits.* New York: John Wiley and Sons, 1999.

Finegan, Andrew. "Soft Systems Methodology: Eliciting Information." *Complexity International,* 1998.

Garvin, David A. *Managing Quality.* New York: Macmillan, 1988.

George, Michael. *Lean Six Sigma: Combining Six Sigma Quality with Lean Speed.* New York: McGraw-Hill, 2002.

Gitlow, H., S. Gitlow, A. Oppenheim, and R. Oppenheim. *Tools and Methods for the Improvement of Quality.* Homeland, IL: Irwin, 1989.

Grant, Eugene L., and Richard S. Leavenworth. *Statistical Quality Control.* New York: McGraw-Hill, 1996.

Hammer, Michael. "Process Management and the Future of Six Sigma." *MIT Sloan Management Review* 43, No. 2, Winter 2002, pp. 26–32.

Harrington, H.J. *Business Process Improvement.* New York: McGraw-Hill, 1991.

Henley, Ernest J., and Hiromitsu Kumamoto. *Reliability Engineering and Risk Assessment.* Englewood Cliffs, NJ: Prentice Hall, 1981.

Hillier, Frederick S., and Gerald J. Lieberman. *Operations Research.* San Francisco: Holden-Day, 1974.

Ishikawa, Kaoru. *Guide to Quality Control.* New York: Asian Productivity Organization, 1985.

Lee, Peter M. *Bayesian Statistics: An Introduction.* New York: Oxford University Press, 1989.

Lee, Yang, and D. Strong. "Process Knowledge and Data Quality Outcomes." *Proc. of 8th International Conference on Information Quality* ICIQ-03, 2003, pp. 96–102.

Lindgren, B.W. *Elements of Decision Theory.* New York: Macmillan.

Lindlay, D.V. *Making Decisions,* 2nd ed. New York: John Wiley and Sons, 1985.

Merli, Giorgio. *Total Manufacturing Management.* Cambridge, MA: Productivity Press, 1990.

Montgomery, Douglas C. *Design and Analysis of Experiments,* 5th ed. New York: John Wiley and Sons, 2000.

Montgomery, Douglas C. *Introduction to Statistical Quality Control,* 4th ed. New York: John Wiley and Sons, 2001.

Ryan, Thomas P. *Statistical Methods for Quality Improvement.* New York: John Wiley and Sons, 1989.

Stamatis, D.H. *Failure Mode and Effects Analysis: FMEA from Theory to Execution,* 2nd ed. Milwaukee: ASQ Quality Press, 2003.

Tummula, V.M. Rao. *Decision Analysis with Business Applications.* New York: Intext Educational Publishers, 1973.

Vander Weil, Scott A., W.T. Tucker, F.W. Faltin, and N. Doganaksoy "Algorithmic Statistical Process Control: Concepts and an Application." *Technometrics* 34, No. 3, August 1992, pp. 298–306.

Index